FOUR STORIES

FOUR STORIES

B Y

SIGRID UNDSET

Translated from the Norwegian by

NAOMI WALFORD

GREENWOOD PRESS, PUBLISHERS
WESTPORT, CONNECTICUT

Library of Congress Cataloging in Publication Data

Undset, Sigrid, 1882-1949.
  Four stories.

    Reprint of the 1st American ed. published by Knopf,
New York.
    CONTENTS: Selma Brøter.--Thjodolf.--Miss Smith-Tellef-
sen.--Simonsen.
  [PZ3.U568Fo   1978] [PT8950.U5] 839.8'2'372 78-16903
  ISBN 0-313-20566-3

Originally published in the Norwegian language by H. Aschehoug &
Co. (W. Nygaard), Oslow, and now included in Volume 5 of *Romaner
Og Fortellinger Fra Nutiden.*

Reprinted with the permission of Alfred A. Knopf, Inc.

Reprinted in 1978 by Greenwood Press, Inc.
51 Riverside Avenue, Westport, CT. 06880

Printed in the United States of America

10 9 8 7 6 5 4 3 2 1

CONTENTS

SELMA BRØTER

THE AFTERNOON sun flooded the engineers' office with gold, and Beate, swinging to and fro on the edge of Stener's drawing-table, narrowed her eyes against the light and said as she dropped her hand to his forehead: "How nice it is in here! What crime have you lazy louts committed to get all the sunshine in life? Tell me that!"

Stener took her arm in both his hands and drew it down against his face. Pushing up her sleeve, he rubbed his mouth and cheek against her soft, fresh skin.

"Do I have to tell you what I've done to keep the sun always shining on me?" He smiled so slyly that she snatched her arm away and slapped his mouth.

"Bad boy!"

"Poor little Beate! Well may you repent. You never knew how awful boys could be. It *is* nice in here," he whispered, and he drew her down from the table onto his knees.

The room was furnished with drawing-tables and, along the walls, yellow-painted cupboards, half open now, with dirty, ink-stained folders and dog-eared drawings bulging out of them. The tables were submerged under untidy papers, bottles of India ink, and worn drawing-instruments; from the corners of the room rolls of carbon paper and sickly-smelling tracing-paper had tumbled out onto the floor. By way of decoration, plans and photographs of turbine installations hung crookedly, in dusty frames, on the harsh blue walls. In the windows, frames of drawings had been set up for photo-printing. They cut off some of the view of the blackish-red warehouse across the street, but above them the sunshine poured in.

Beate Nordahl was fresh and young and soft. Her features were not particularly good: she had a round face with a dumpy little nose, but her mouth was sweet and innocent and there were deep dimples beside it. Her skin was a clear pink-and-white, her forehead dazzling against her almost black and rather bushy hair, and beneath the coal-black brows and long lashes her light gray eyes looked large and brilliant.

She was always cheerful and good-humored too, with him. Sweet and gentle and warm and affectionate. Never in all the months they had been engaged had he seen her otherwise. It still seemed to him extraordinary that she should be the same person as that sulky little Miss Nordahl who had been in the same office with him for two years: that capable, unapproachable, abrupt, and downright person whom no one else in the firm ever really learned to know.

Then one day all the office staff had been invited to

the house of the former accountant, who had left to get married. By way of thanks to her colleagues for the wedding present they had given her she asked them to a party, and afterward Stener Gundersen took Miss Nordahl home. Thenceforward, as if by chance, they always left the office together; and how all the rest had come about, neither of them really knew. Beate indeed declared, looking back, that she had been in love with him ever since he first came to the office: "Without my knowing it, of course. Or at least, perhaps I wasn't really in love with you. But I always had the feeling that you were quite, quite different from all the other men I'd met; you were the first real *man*."

Stener said nothing like that, for he remembered very clearly what his first impression of her had been; and it was the more miraculous that things should have turned out as they had. And when he recalled his first two years here in Christiania—how horrible and dreary the place had seemed, how poor and homeless he had felt, how disappointed both in his work, which was monotonous, almost mechanical, and in life, in which he could see no purpose—then he would take Beate in his arms and crush her almost to suffocation.

Sometimes she clung to him and returned his caress wildly, furiously. Her childlike little face went white, distorted with passion, and she whispered between endless, dragging kisses: "Suppose we'd never found each other, Stener. Or fancy if one of us died—"

All this ran through his mind as he watched the sunshine striking sparks from her dark hair. And he believed she was thinking of the same thing, for she whispered: "Poor thing!"

But when he asked: "Who's a poor thing?" and raised her face to his, it was smiling and calm and rosy-red.

"Miss Brøter, of course."

"Oh, I don't know," he remarked thoughtfully.

"Oh, yes!" Beate laughed. "Poor Miss Brøter. I think it must be miserable to know it all so well in theory—all the awfulness of men—"

"Shame on you, Beate!" said Stener, making a shocked face.

"But don't you see, they must be quite obsessed by this thing that they're shut out of? They *must* be, because they go on and on about it so. Nobody's ever tried any awfulness with them, and in their hearts they resent this, and they're inquisitive and they keep harping on it and sharing what scraps of knowledge they've picked up at second hand. Like Miss Jahn and Miss Brøter. I tell you, hardly a day passes without their having some fearful tale to tell and shudder at— usually in the lunch break. In those days—before, I mean—*I* never wanted to hear about that sort of

6

thing; I wanted to believe it was all beautiful, all the
—all the secret part of life. I could never have
brought myself to chatter about it. And now I think
it's so sad that anyone should . . ." She kissed his
forehead.

"Anyhow, it's a good thing she's got rid of that
waster of a brother at last," said Stener. "And now
that she's moved to a pension, who knows? Perhaps
even Selma Brøter can find herself a sweetheart."

"I wish she could. But I won't believe it till I see it.
There's a sort of indescribable something about her,
as if the Lord had written on her forehead that she
was to be returned to Him in the fullness of time as
untouched by earthly love as when she came into the
world. Her brothers and sister must have felt that;
look how they left her to take care of their mother,
and then afterward brother Ludvig. That beast—!"

Stener rocked her on his knee and laughed.

"Oh, you can laugh. But don't you think it would
have been better if *she* had robbed the till, or perhaps had a baby? Then the cousin in Cape Town
would have offered *her* the free passage out and a
good job and a fine new start in life and all the rest
of it."

"I wouldn't be too sure. It's different when it's a
woman that runs off the rails."

"Yes, yes, that's true. Isn't it damnable, though,
that people have to get up to something like that be-

fore anybody will give them a helping hand? If only the cousin had taken that Ludvig creature a bit earlier! Poor Miss Brøter, she used to cry her eyes out over that boy.

"And yet you know I envied Miss Brøter once, before I had you," she whispered down to him. "At least she had someone to cry over and be fond of—when he promised to mend his ways, and she thought everything was going to be all right. There was someone who needed her—whom she could love. I had nobody."

"My sweet!" He rocked her back and forth.

"Did you hear that? It was five o'clock striking. Let me go—ouch, are you mad? They probably suspect something already, now that we've taken to turning up before the others. No, Stener, let go. Supposing somebody comes." She tore herself free and collected his rough drafts from the desk.

"Well, have a nice evening with the aunts!"

"Ha, ha. I expect I shall get your sofa cushion finished anyway. Be a good boy and give her a nice time. Remember to buy sweets for her—a big bag of them. Give her some cold supper afterward, with beer, and punch with the coffee. Then she'll feel she's been on a real binge."

Stener nodded and Beate nodded back vigorously from the door—then turned to go to meet him again. But at that moment Jørgensen came in.

8

When Beate entered the correspondence office, Selma Brøter was standing in front of the little looking-glass above the basin, tidying her hair. She had been to the hairdresser.

"Why, here already, Miss Nordahl!"

"Yes, Mr. Gundersen had a long letter that has to catch the Stockholm train. Now then, let's look at you!"

Beate walked round her admiringly.

"How well that hair style suits you. And what a pretty blouse—did you buy it ready-made? Oh, Miss Rasmussen made it. How clever she must be—it's charming. Shall I help you—?"

She helped Selma Brøter to button an overall over the pink silk blouse. Then she sat down at her typewriter, slipped in the paper, and began on the letter to Stockholm. But when she came to an almost illegible passage she subsided into her own thoughts.

She wanted to lay her cheek down on the scrawled sheets and kiss his writing—that appalling scribble with its erasures and corrections and spelling mistakes on every other line, such as she had inwardly fumed over every day for two years. She smiled over at Miss Brøter.

"Really, Mr. Gundersen's writing! And do you know he spells 'where' without an h and 'were' with one?"

She was unaware that she said this as if it were both

9

admirable and touching of Gundersen to have such peculiar spelling. And Miss Brøter didn't notice it either; she replied, quite piqued on his behalf: "Oh, but I think all engineers spell badly. It's not their business to bother about things like that when they're so busy. It's only reasonable that they should leave such things to us.

"Mr. Gundersen's *so* kind. None of the other engineers are nearly so considerate. He never gives us any work after seven o'clock if he can help it. And just think how he stayed late in the evenings to help you with the costing—"

"Yes, you're quite right; Mr. Gundersen is nice," said Beate. She smiled again. "But he writes like a great schoolboy; that's all I meant."

She swung herself to and fro on her revolving chair, with her toe braced against the floor, feeling a small, voluptuous pleasure in the tensing of the muscles in her healthy young body. And she smiled again.

She let her hand rest on the keys of the typewriter, playing on them as if they were piano keys, caressingly, without pressing them down. S-t-e-n-e-r. Over and over again.

Miss Brøter didn't seem in the mood for work either. She stared through the window into the narrow, dark back yard. Both machines were silent.

The wearing clatter of two typewriters had tormented Beate for two years. Now she almost liked it, and liked the dark little cubbyhole they had been given, so that the noise should not disturb others in the office. Suddenly she knew that one day, when she came to leave here, both she and Stener would be sorry to say good-by to this room where he had sat faithfully, evening after evening, helping her with her figures. The room from which they had walked out into blue, magical spring nights—out into the town, which both of them had once hated because they had been lonely and homeless and filled with longing amid its noise and crowds. It had grown infinitely dear to them; it was their only confidant. The town with the quiet streets on its outskirts, where the gas lamps shone soft and golden under airy domes of young foliage along the garden fences, and the sky rose lofty and deep blue above it all. The town that lay sparkling far below his attic room when they clung together by the window at night, looking down.

Everything, everything was different now. What joy had she known before? Reckoning from payday to payday how much she could put in the bank that month; dreaming of the time when she would have saved enough to go out into the world—and what did that mean but going to and from work in an even bigger town, where she would feel yet stranger and lonelier? Now she was drawing money from the bank, buying "things for the house" and storing them in her bed-sitting-room; then saving again and paying installments on a birchwood corner cupboard. She didn't want to take out all her money, for they were going to spend their honeymoon in Paris, and there would be lots of things she would want to bring home from there. But she would have to withdraw something for those old branched candlesticks; they were to be a Christmas present for Stener, and would stand on his writing-table. The white china lamps that she had had set aside for her at the junkshop could be paid for on Saturday when she received her salary. She had thought of the shades she would make for them: bucket-shaped ones of white silk with little red hearts appliquéd on them—thin silk, to let the light through. It would be fun to make a whole set of mats for the dining-room, with red hearts on white linen. Or perhaps green four-leafed clovers. She would ask Stener and get him to help her with the design.

Everything was fun now. She had suddenly become good friends with everyone at the office; she showed the other women her needlework and made them talk. There was really so much good in them all —and so much that was funny, too: things to laugh at afterward with Stener. She was quite looking forward to the aunts this evening. Before, they had merely irritated her because they were so stupid and, as it were, fossilized, and never understood a thing. But now that she could tell Stener about them afterward until he laughed himself sick, she felt that in a way they were rather sweet.

Suddenly irritated by the mess her desk was in, she began brushing away the crumbs of India rubber that were scattered round her machine. This evening she would get rid of all the inkspots and put fresh blotting-paper on the blotter.

She drew toward her the vase that held Stener's roses, and buried her face in them, smiling happily.

"What beautiful roses," Miss Brøter said. "I've been admiring them."

"Yes, aren't they wonderful? I couldn't resist—I just had to buy them. I must be mad."

"My goodness! I wonder—could you possibly spare me one for this evening? It would be so kind."

Beate sat with the vase between her hands and her face plunged in the flowers. Give away his roses . . .

Then she began to look among them, and picked out the two loveliest: they were half-opened buds, one white and one deep red.

It was that feeling she always had of being too happy. It made her almost afraid, and impelled her to buy her right to happiness by being kind. It was she who had refused to disappoint the old aunts, she who had suggested to Stener that he should take Miss Brøter to the theater this evening, with the tickets he'd been given by an actress cousin.

So she smiled, and with a feeling of making sacrifice to the goddesses of fate, she went over and fastened the roses carefully to Selma Brøter's pink blouse.

2

MISS BRØTER had had a *wonderful* time.

"And how charming Mr. Gundersen's cousin is!" she said next day in the lunch break, when all the ladies gathered in the accounts office. "You can't think how pretty. In the third act when she wears boy's clothes—I've never seen anything so enchanting. And she sings delightfully."

"She didn't get very good press notices," said Miss Horn, the new accountant. "She's never made a real hit. And I don't think she is so very pretty—just passable."

"Oh, she's pretty, all right," said Miss Jahn, the cashier. "They say she's terribly flighty. I can quite see why men find her so attractive. Little baggage! I wonder whether Mr. Gundersen isn't a bit smitten—"

"No, I'm quite sure he's not," Miss Brøter said warmly. "She's engaged, he told me—engaged to Birger Tande."

"Is that the man at Andersen and Smith's?" asked Miss Horn. "I know there's a Tande there. I met him in the country one summer, and he knew lots of people like that."

"No, no, the actor," said Miss Brøter, almost indignantly. "He had a small part last night. Nice-looking boy."

"Oh, that's right," Miss Horn rejoined. "I believe I remember him. They give him the walk-on parts, don't they?"

"Oh, well, he's quite young, you know. And then afterward we had a wonderful supper. I must say Mr. Gundersen's a charming host. So attentive. You'd never think it to see him in the office—he's always so quiet—but dear me! Yes, it was really lovely."

Beate, who was sitting on the windowsill eating a sandwich, smiled to herself. Stener seemed to have done well. Yes, he was sweet and kind. . . .

Miss Kittelsen, who as the youngest in the office had the duty of making the tea, asked if anybody wanted any more. Beate held out her cup.

"You and I will be getting tickets next week, Miss Kittelsen. Mr. Gundersen asked me this morning if I thought you'd like to go; he's going to ask his cousin."

"Oh, how lovely! And how kind of Mr. Gundersen."

Beate smiled contentedly. She had just invented this, because Miss Kittelsen was nice and never had any fun. She was a tall, fair, very young girl with something peculiarly quiet and distinguished about her. She lived with her mother, who was a widow with several younger children and kept a draper's shop somewhere out among the new streets in the Frogner district.

Gundersen came in just then to fetch a brief case, and Miss Kittelsen ran radiantly up to him.

"Thank you so very much, Mr. Gundersen. It's most terribly kind of you. I'm looking forward to it tremendously."

"I told her you'd promised to get us both tickets for the theater next week," said Beate gravely. Only in her eyes was there a glint of a smile. "We're both looking forward to it."

"Oh, not at all—I'm glad—" he stammered.

Beate put down her cup and left the room. She was standing in the passage laughing when he came out.

"Oh, what an ass you looked, Stener!" She put her arms round his neck and kissed him.

"How was I to know what you were up to? I thought you were coming with me."

"Not at all. I shall take Miss Kittelsen the evening you have to go to the Polytechnic. When you and I can be together, we can surely find something better to do than go to the theater—hi, let go! Are you crazy?" A door farther down the passage opened. "The director!" She ran into her own office.

. . .

A day or two after this, Miss Brøter told Beate that Mr. Gundersen had invited them both to his room one evening. He was going to ask his cousin and her fiancé too.

"I think it might be great fun, but I didn't give a definite answer. It can't matter, though, can it, with so many of us there? Do you think it would be wrong—?"

"Surely not. There'll be three of us women. There can't be anything wrong about that." Beate's face was innocent and grave.

"Then I'll accept for both of us. I think it will be tremendously interesting to meet Miss Gundersen and Mr. Tande, don't you? She's so charming. Such fun meeting artists and people like that. Did you know Mr. Gundersen has a piano? He told me. He's buying it on the installment plan. Isn't it amusing? Perhaps Miss Gundersen will sing."

"Fancy that—a piano. I can see we're going to enjoy ourselves."

"So interesting to go to one of these Bohemian parties. I wonder what his place is like. I'm sure he's fixed it up very comfortably."

"Yes, I expect he has," Beate agreed as gravely as ever.

"I believe Mr. Gundersen really likes going about and meeting nice girls and so on. Haven't you noticed how he's taken to waiting for us in the evenings when we leave work?"

Beate didn't answer. She was really grave now. Miss Brøter had formed the tiresome habit of waiting for Beate in the evenings, for the sake of company, so that Beate and Stener were obliged to go with her all the way to her pension. The only fun to be had out of this—touching hands surreptitiously, without her noticing—soon grew tame. And that it should happen now, on these lovely autumn evenings . . . However, once they'd got rid of her they could stroll to their hearts' content, and they had their long evenings together in his room, so it didn't really matter. It would have been a shame to grudge her that little bit of pleasure, when she so much liked having someone to see her home.

"Yes, and whenever he comes in here he stays and talks. My dear, haven't you noticed? Not surprising, really; we're the ones he has most to do with. And Miss Jahn and Miss Horn are rather older, so he probably doesn't care to talk to them so much."

"No, probably not," Beate agreed with a smile. It had never occurred to her to think of Miss Brøter as being any younger than the other two: they were all between thirty and forty. And Beate was twenty-three.

Mr. Gundersen really did give a party for the ladies one Saturday evening. Miss Kittelsen was also invited, and a very pleasant party it was. The cousin was most agreeable, quite ready to sing and play the whole evening, and Tande was a very nice, quiet young man. Beate Nordahl undertook to make the coffee and Miss Kittelsen laid the table, while Miss Brøter monopolized Mr. Gundersen.

Later in the evening, Beate and Stener stood together for a moment by the open window, and she whispered: "Isn't it fun? It's as if we were married and giving our first party."

"Yes," he whispered back. "And so we are, aren't we? Only the others don't know that this is *your* home."

She laughed.

"Do you suppose that Selma Brøter and Anni Kittelsen would ever come if they had known?"

3

SELMA BRØTER was sitting by the window darning a pair of white skiing-mittens when someone knocked at the door. It was the pharmacist.

"I thought I'd look in for a chat with you, Miss Broter," he said, and he sat down unasked on the little divan bed across the corner, under the twilight lamp. "How warm and snug it is in here!" He stretched out his legs, tucked his thumbs into the armholes of his waistcoat, whistled, and stared at the ceiling. "And you've put water on to boil, too; good girl! I had a feeling when I was up in my room—I said to myself: 'Miss Brøter's making some coffee for you.'" He gave a whinnying laugh.

"Then you were wrong, Mr. Møller. That water's for washing my skiing-cap."

"You don't mean that, Miss Brøter; you have too good a heart. The only thing about me is a little drop of Benedictine—as good as we chemists can make it. But all things at thy feet I lay—" he chanted.

"And I haven't any cream."

"Allow me! Just lend me your little pot—there it is, on *top* of the bedside table!" He snatched up the little Chinese cream jug and rose.

"Oh, very well," Selma Brøter said, smiling a little.

Poor Møller—he wasn't so bad really. It would be a shame to grudge him a drop of coffee. Not that she approved of the way both the men and the women in this pension had of sitting in one another's rooms. On the contrary, she found it most distasteful. But poor Møller was somehow different, for he had no idea that there was anything wrong in strolling in whenever he felt like it.

She knew the poor man was rather smitten with her. But surely he couldn't be getting any ideas? He must realize that he was too old. He had a potbelly and a bald patch, and practically no eyes behind the gold-rimmed glasses. And he was fat and pasty-faced, and reminded one of those thick white maggots one finds under stones. And he had absolutely no manners. He was common, but good-natured. In fact, she quite liked him. It wasn't his fault that he'd had no upbringing.

Moreover, he came from her part of the country. She remembered both him and his brothers and sisters from the time she was a little girl. Every year on his holiday he went back to Toten, and it was nice to hear news of it, of the new people on the Brøter farm and of how they had improved it.

Selma sighed heavily. If her father had been another sort of man, her own life might have turned out very differently.

But Møller, now; surely he couldn't have any hopes of that sort? She smiled. She knew perfectly well that she had never given him any encouragement; yet she couldn't bring herself to be positively unfriendly either.

The coffee was simmering over the spirit lamp that stood on a corner of the marble-topped washstand, and she went to the window to pull down the roller blind, but paused and looked out. Snow was still whirling down in big flakes, and the kitchen window on the opposite side of the courtyard showed only as a blurred red patch of light. Tomorrow the going might be quite heavy. She smiled again: she would have some liqueur to take along with her now. Møller always left the bottle with her when he contributed liqueur to the coffee. "Put a nipple on it," he used to say, "and take a pull during the night. Much better than bromide or veronal." Yes, he was a bit vulgar.

But it would be a shame to refuse him when he so much enjoyed coming. And she fancied she had a good influence on him; the rest of his acquaintances were probably not up to much. And hers was a cosy little room.

She pulled down the blind and lit the pink hanging lamp, then straightened the photographs on the little table by the window. They were of her mother, her brother Ludvig—the failure—and her brother Henrik, who had been the hope of the family. (He had been second mate aboard a big Tønsberg vessel, but had drowned in the Pacific four years earlier.) Also of her sister Alvilde and husband, Dahl, the attorney of Mo in Ranen.

There was no picture of her father. Old Brøter had been a real rustic who by some odd chance had married the daughter of a government official. She had been anemic and bilious and was always difficult to get on with; and as she became increasingly dissatisfied with her husband—who didn't understand her, and whose very nature constituted a perpetual torment to her nerves and mind—she grew more and more sickly and fretful. The day she discovered that the maid was pregnant by her husband, she left home with all the children, and since then Brøter had been dead to her. He had to provide for her, but those matters were handled by an attorney.

Selma had been twelve when her parents separated, and she had never seen her father since. She pictured him as her mother had taught her to do. In fact, Selma had seen everything through her mother's eyes, all the years she lived with her. When Brøter's contribution diminished, as one child after another reached the age of eighteen, she had regarded it as quite natural that she as the eldest daughter should sacrifice herself for the family. Henrik helped a little, and sent money home, and Mrs. Brøter had fifteen hundred crowns a year from her husband as long as she was alive. But Alvilde, the beauty of the family, was musical, and her talent had to be developed. Luckily she married well. But then there was Ludvig. He had been a beautiful, rather delicate child, and was therefore spoiled. He had a good brain too, and was talented in so many different directions that he found it hard to settle down to any one thing. Yet it was on Ludvig that his mother and Selma had pinned all their hopes. Something would come of that boy, they agreed; and with that reflection they concluded all their long conversations about his little transgressions and excellent qualities. On her deathbed, Mrs. Brøter entrusted her favorite child to Selma, and

Selma, with her mother's hand in hers, had promised to sacrifice herself for Ludvig.

Selma paused with the photograph in her hand. She had tried to erase the memory of that dreadful time. She dimly recalled a block of offices in Lower Palace Street, and a white marble stairway. With the clarity of a vivid dream she could see a landing with blue walls and a reddish-brown glazed door opposite. On the pane was inscribed "Herbert Klampenborg, Advocate of the Supreme Court." On the wall to the left of this door, in black letters, was painted "A La Parisienne. Mrs. Bergliot Arnesen, Ladies' Hairdressing and Beauty Treatment," and a big arrow pointing down a corridor.

It seemed odd that she should retain so vivid a memory of that landing, where she had paused and braced herself to go on, to climb a floor higher to Ludvig's employers. For of that place she remembered nothing at all.

Of all the other things—the arrest, the rooms and figures pertaining to mysteries called law and law courts—she retained only a vague impression, as of machinery glimpsed in a dark room. But the black doorway of that room gaped at her, and through it Ludvig would have to pass for the machinery to seize and crush him. She had wept; a dire disgrace had overhung them all, and there had been notices in the papers—no name was mentioned, but it was Ludvig.

When things were at their worst, the boy was released. His chiefs withdrew the charge against him; the cousin in Africa made good the deficit, stretched forth a long arm and plucked Ludvig away. And she, confused, bewildered, and mentally bludgeoned, had landed in this pension.

Forlorn and grief-stricken she had sat in this lonely little room, afraid of everybody; afraid of the strangers whom she saw at meals and heard racketing in the rooms and passages around her. Møller had been a good friend in those days. He had been marvelously kind. It would be mean to show him the door now, just because circumstances had altered and brought her as good a life as other girls had, and friends whom she preferred to him.

She hummed softly as she took the coffee off the spirit lamp and put on more water for her washing. Mr. Møller certainly deserved a cup of coffee now and then. She laid the table attractively and set the vase of preserved ferns in the middle.

"Yum, yum!" Møller said, sniffing the aroma of coffee when he came in with the cream jug in one hand, a promising paper bag in the other, and the liqueur bottle under his arm. And oh dear, there he went, shaking snow and water off himself all over her floor.

"Oof, what lousy weather! Cosy in here, though." He stretched himself out on the sofa and filled cups and glasses while she arranged the cakes on a plate. "*Skål!*"

Selma sat down and tasted the liqueur.

"So you're going out winter-sporting tomorrow, are you? Ah, you girls—never cold, are you? That's the fire in your veins. Ha ha! Is it your poor little engineer again?" And Møller winked.

"'If you mean Mr. Gundersen, yes, I'm going with him."

"Poor boy. It's cruel of you, Miss Brøter, if you're not serious about him."

"Don't be so absurd."

"Don't be so absurd," he mimicked. "Oh, you're a dangerous girl, you are—trifling with men's affections. You can all do that, we know. First poor old me and now this whippersnapper. Variety's the spice of life, I suppose!"

"How can you talk like that, Mr. Møller! You can't pretend for a moment that I've ever led *you* on."

"Oh, no, of course not. It's not your fault you're such a charming, delightful little lady. The ladies are never to blame."

"And as for Mr. Gundersen," she went on hastily, "I've never heard of such a thing. Why, he must be three if not four years younger than me—perhaps five. Besides, we're not always alone together. Tomorrow Miss Nordahl's coming. As a matter of fact, she usually does. It seems very natural to me, as we're in the same office, that we should get together and enjoy ourselves. You know perfectly well I'd never flirt with him—the very idea! One does have some sense of decency. Such a thing would never enter my head."

Møller merely nodded and pulled an ugly face.

"I can't think why it is that a man and a woman can't meet without people seeing that sort of thing in it," Selma pursued, with some heat. "Surely they can be friends?"

"Poor boy, that's all I say."

"Oh, you're impossible!"

But she was crimson in the face, and found it hard to conceal her agitation.

Møller observed her stealthily as, without asking leave, he lit a cigar. Perhaps this was a dangerous dose to administer—worse than liqueur. Oh, well, she'd sober up again; she might have an emotional hang-over next day, maybe, but nothing serious. And for the moment it made the poor soul blissfully happy.

"Anyway, I shall ask Mr. Gundersen in to coffee one Saturday, and then you'll see what a nice, sensible young man he is. *He'd* never have such ideas. And Miss Nordahl—now there's someone you'll fall head-over-heels in love with at once, Mr. Møller! I know there's nothing so dangerous for elderly gentlemen as girls of that age."

Møller had his own thoughts on the subject of old maids and boys, but said nothing.

While he was shaving in his room—for he was going out that evening—his friend Arvesen came in.

"Damned if I know how you can bear to spend so much time with her," said Arvesen.

"There's nothing wrong with Miss Brøter," Møller said gravely as he scraped his face. "I like going there. We're from the same district, remember. I knew her mother. Good God, when I think of her slaving all those years for that old hag . . . And that waster of a brother. Selma's the only one of the Brøters who takes after the old man: kind and loyal and hard-working—likes a bit of fun but never gets any—starved and withered. Hell, if I was quite sure she'd refuse me I'd propose to her. Nobody else will, and it's damned hard luck on a woman to be an old maid without even having had the chance to turn somebody down."

4

JUST after Christmas, Beate Nordahl suddenly left the firm, and a couple of days later engagement cards from her and Mr. Gundersen appeared on every desk.

Miss Horn and Miss Jahn had guessed it all along, they said. And they asked Miss Brøter at once whether she had been in the secret. They hadn't exactly said anything, Miss Brøter answered, but of course she had always known. Miss Horn asked how long Miss Brøter thought it had been going on. Oh, not long, Selma believed. Were they terribly in love? Did they cuddle? Had they been good company? Then they discussed Beate's qualities and shortcomings, and Gundersen's future. He had told Miss Horn in answer to her question that they would be getting married "fairly soon." But surely they wouldn't be so mad. When they'd thought it over they would come to their senses. Miss Nordahl's family in Kragerø, with whom she was now staying to learn something about housekeeping and to make her trousseau, would be sure to talk her out of it. They would have to wait at least a couple of years. Did Miss Nordahl write to Miss Brøter? Did Miss Brøter still see anything of Mr. Gundersen after office hours?

But little Anni Kittelsen soon put a stop to that game. It was when Miss Horn said to Miss Brøter one day: "You know, at first I was sure that it was to be *you* and Mr. Gundersen! He was paying you such a lot of attention at one time—"

Selma said only: "Good gracious me, what nonsense."

But when she had gone, Anni Kittelsen rose up

with blazing eyes and said, right in Miss Horn's face: "You ought to be ashamed of yourself!"

And Miss Horn did look ashamed—for a moment. Then she gave a provoking laugh.

"Now, now don't get so excited, my dear little Miss Kittelsen! I don't know what you mean. But one thing I *must* say," she hastened to add, with the greatest indignation. "I think Mr. Gundersen has behaved disgracefully. Just think how he used to pay court to her. And Miss Nordahl's no better. They both used her as a screen, that's all."

"I don't believe it. I won't believe it of either of them," Anni Kittelsen broke in.

"Well, it would be odd if those two were the only people in the office who didn't realize. The woman was crazy about him. At least Miss Nordahl would see it, you'd think—probably she did, and thought it was all a huge joke."

Miss Kittelsen had wrapped up her half-eaten sandwich and put it in her overall pocket. Now she picked up her teacup and went toward the door.

"I've only one thing to say to you, Miss Horn, if you're interested in my opinion, and that is that you're the most spiteful, vulgar, coarse creature I could ever have imagined. So now you know. Goodby."

With that, she went into the little room where she made out her invoices, and shut the door after her.

Miss Horn gave a sneering laugh and muttered something about insolent little girls. But from that day onward Miss Brøter was left in peace.

The ladies of the office were to experience sensation after sensation during that winter and the spring that followed.

First, Mr. Gundersen and Miss Nordahl were married three weeks after announcing their engagement. No one knew anything of it until one Monday morning another set of cards announced that the event had taken place. When asked about it, Gundersen explained that Beate and he had been married on Saturday—it was a civil wedding—after he left the office, and that they had dined at Frognerseteren with their witnesses afterward. The couple stayed until Sunday evening at a skiing-hut belonging to one of his friends —he had to confess this, because someone from Miss Jahn's pension had seen Gundersen in Nordmarka that Sunday, with a lady—and they had rented a two-room flat with a kitchen and maid's room at the top of Terese Street; for the present they would not have a maid, and Beate had found some translating and typing work to do at home; the typewriter was hired.

The office staff got up a collection among themselves and gave the newly married couple a clock. They were then invited to supper.

Even Miss Horn had to admit that the Gundersens' place was "an idyll," although she didn't think the sitting-room showed a scrap of taste. Corner cupboard, chest of drawers, and mirror, of birchwood in the Empire style; two different armchairs in peasant rococo; a couch, full of cushions and covered with flowered cretonne; and home-woven curtains. And it was sheer affectation to go and hang up those two huge photographs of naked, writhing men, even if they *were* by Michaelangelo.

But she had to confess that the kitchen was simply charming. Gundersen had chosen the colors, said Beate proudly. The walls were pale yellow, the plate racks, bench-cupboard, and other furniture green, and in one corner there was a little dining-table, with two cushioned chairs. The crockery on the shelves and all the cloths and curtains were white and scarlet; tin and copper vessels shone brightly, and over the table hung photographs of Dutch paintings: girls peeling potatoes, and so on. They had all their meals there, Mrs. Gundersen said, and it was really so snug that Miss Horn was sorry there was no room for them all to have supper there that evening.

Beate used the maid's room as a study, and had her typewriter in there. The bedroom was not on view, but Miss Jahn, who asked to go into it for a wash, reported that the furniture was painted white—it was the cheap sort made by convicts—and the loose covers were blue.

The couple seemed delighted with it all, and Beate

readily explained to her guests how she organized her day's work; they had to admit that she was more domesticated and practical than they had ever thought possible. So for the present it was agreed that the Gundersens, with their twenty-four hundred crowns and two rooms, had built themselves a delightful little nest.

But two months later Miss Horn announced at the lunch break that she had met Mrs. Gundersen in Torv Street, and that it showed *quite plainly*. But of course Miss Horn—and Miss Jahn too—had suspected something when those two rushed off and got married in that headlong fashion. But they hadn't wanted to mention it; after all, it *might* have been a mistake, and then of course it would have been very wrong to hint at such a thing. But now Miss Horn was quite certain: Mrs. Gundersen was going to have a baby. Miss Horn had even walked a little way with her, and poor Mrs. Gundersen had been quite embarrassed and awkward.

This sensational news was discussed at length and in detail. The previous topic—the fact that Miss Kittelsen's mother, who ran the draper's shop, had had to settle with her creditors—was put entirely in the shade. Nobody talked any more about the idyllic little nest in Terese Street. On the contrary, they thought it was all such a shame— Miss Horn was sorriest for Mr. Gundersen, but not Miss Jahn—well, a little, perhaps, though a man had to take the consequences of his own actions—but, oh, that poor, pretty little girl!

Well, she wasn't all that pretty, declared Miss Horn. She never had been. It was her coloring and her health and so on that made her seem so. And now she was sallow and peaky, and looked old. But it was her own doing. If a woman had so little self-respect . . . For a man to try for what he wanted—well, it wasn't *right,* of course, but that was how they all were. Miss Horn knew that from her own experience.

"And yet you know I just can't understand how any engaged couple can let it go so far," Miss Jahn said. "How they can have so little regard for each other . . ."

Miss Kittelsen gave no opinion at lunch. After her rudeness to Miss Horn she had been punished by being completely ignored by the others. But since her mother's misfortune, Miss Horn had taken her back into favor and been overwhelmingly amiable. However, Miss Kittelsen continued to be curt and abrupt with her. But to Miss Jahn, whom Miss Kittelsen liked because she was good-natured at heart, she said what she thought.

She was ashamed and angry to reflect that for months she had been daily in the company of such people; and shocked and disillusioned. If Mr. Gun-

dersen and Miss Nordahl were like that, whom *could*
one trust? She dared not tell even her mother about it.
To think he had had the impudence to invite her to
his room with his—his . . . for Beate might have
been that even then, for all they knew. Miss Kittelsen
was tearful with indignation. And she drew Miss
Jahn's attention to the way she treated Mr. Gundersen now. Not a word should he get out of her beyond
what their work required. On the Wednesday before
Easter, when she went round saying good-by before
going on holiday, she neither wished him a happy
Easter nor shook hands with him; never again would
she take Mr. Gundersen's hand.

Selma Brøter said not one word on the subject.

However, in time even that topic was exhausted;
especially after Mr. Gundersen had said quite uncon-
cernedly, in answer to inquiries from the cashier and
the accountant—how was his wife, and wasn't it too
bad of her not to look in at the office and greet her old
friends, and so on—that Beate wasn't very well just
now. But wouldn't they call on her, perhaps on Saturday, and have coffee?

Miss Kittelsen and Miss Brøter declined with
thanks, but Miss Horn and Miss Jahn accepted. Beate
received them, radiant and quite unembarrassed, in a
black maternity frock with a little white collar. The
coffee table was delightfully arranged, the home-made
cakes were delicious, and the flat was warm and sunny.

It was one of the first days in May, and the balcony door stood open. Beate displayed three green boxes filled with soil in which she was going to plant flowers, and two for the kitchen window for parsley and chives; then she introduced them to her roses, which were shooting strongly, each with its little yellow stick label beside it.

Later, Miss Brøter turned up after all. But she sat and said very little as she drank Beate's second brew of coffee.

When the guests were leaving, Beate managed a few words alone with Miss Brøter in the hall.

"Couldn't you look in sometimes in the evenings? Stener tells me it's no good his asking you, but we would be so glad to see you. We three used to have such good times together in the old days. Just let Stener know on the morning of a day when you've got nothing better to do, and he'll bring you back with him in the evening. Please do!"

Miss Brøter thanked her and said she would like to come very much, and that she would see. However, for the time being she didn't go, although Stener invited her several times.

After that coffee party, Miss Horn and Miss Jahn decided that the Gundersens must have been engaged for a fairly long time, which could be regarded as an extenuating circumstance; because Mrs. Gundersen had a tablecloth, embroidered in Venetian stitch,

which she had made during her engagement, and it
represented at least four months' work. With that,
the Gundersen question was finally closed.

They received a fresh supply of conversation material immediately afterward. This time it was Selma
Brøter's affairs. Mr. Dahl, her brother-in-law, the advocate at Mo in Ranen, died suddenly of heart failure, and her sister was left very badly off. Dahl's life
had been insured, but a certain amount had been bor-
rowed on the policy; Selma didn't know exactly how
it was, but there wouldn't be much left for poor
Alvilde.

Selma Brøter seemed quite out of her mind. She
could talk of nothing but her sister's affairs. Whenever anyone came into the office, she began asking
questions and demanding explanations about inher-
itance and insurance and so on. The new secretary
was driven nearly mad by having to hear over and
over again about the distress at Mo, and at the pension they shunned Selma like the plague for the same
reason. Møller was kind and patient, but he had little
knowledge of business, and anyhow was often out in
the evenings during that time.

But Miss Horn was extremely kind; she was also a
capable person, and rather enjoyed playing provi-
dence. So she sat with Selma after office hours, reading
through letters from the attorney and from the sister,
dictating replies, asking questions and making Selma

explain, and drawing up balance sheets on large pieces of paper. And Selma was somehow soothed by being in the company of this authoritative personality.

But at home in the evenings, when she had drunk her tea alone in the pension dining-room—long after the others had finished supper—and entered her lonely room, she lay down on her bed and cried and cried. . . .

She took out the bundle of Alvilde's despairing letters and went through them, beginning with the frightful telegram; she read them all and wept even more bitterly. And it was just as terrible and incomprehensible now as it had been that Sunday morning when the telegram came and she threw herself down and prayed to God—as if that could alter the fact— that Alfred might not, should not be dead.

She hadn't known her brother-in-law very well, but had worshipped him because he was Alvilde's husband; and he had been madly in love with Alvilde and showered her with beautiful presents while they were engaged. Alvilde had not been a good correspondent, but it had never occurred to Selma to doubt that she and her husband got on well together and were happy, and she knew that Alvilde had a fine house up there, and lived in style. She had always taken it for granted that her sister should be petted and made much of; thus it had been at home, and

she assumed that it would always be so wherever Alvilde went—Alvilde who was so beautiful and clever.
And in hours of sadness, when it seemed to Selma that
things had gone badly for the rest of them, her consolation had been—and she thanked God for it—that
Alvilde at any rate was well off.

And now she was a widow, and expecting a child as
well. And Miss Horn said she wouldn't have more
than forty crowns a month at most to live on—unless
she started a business with her money, as Miss Horn
advised. But it was not easy to find anything suitable.

It was decided that Alvilde should move to Christiania in the autumn and live with Selma, who luckily was in a good position now and could support her.
They would rent a small flat and for the time being
Alvilde would keep house for them both, while they
waited to see how things turned out.

5

THEY moved into two rooms and a kitchen up near
Sankthans Hill. Alvilde had kept some of her furniture, and Selma had bought herself a couch bed and
an American rocking-chair. She already possessed a
chest of drawers.

At first they had to have a girl in in the mornings.
Alvilde was too wretchedly unwell to manage any-

thing more than cooking the dinner. Selma washed up before going back to the office, and got supper when she came home at night. And indeed she quite enjoyed having a little domestic work to do once more. Although she was sometimes a little tired at the end of the day, there was some truth in what she had once read: that a change of work was a rest.

This arrangement was to be temporary. Once Alvilde had had her baby and was strong again, she would of course take over all the housework, or at any rate enough of it to ensure that Selma did no more than she wanted to. Also, Alvilde was going to give piano lessons. At the moment they had to manage on Selma's hundred crowns a month and Alvilde's twenty-seven; for that was all she received when her affairs were wound up.

The worst part of it from Selma's point of view was that Alvilde was terribly difficult to get on with these days. One couldn't complain, for of course it must be quite dreadful for her. Selma marveled that anyone could endure it at all. With all Alvilde had been through—in her condition, too—and having been so pampered, she must find poverty horribly hard to bear. She was so irritable that Selma hardly dared open her mouth; often she flared up and seemed quite beside herself, though Selma had no idea what had annoyed her.

On Saturday, for instance, they were to have

minced fish and rice fritters, and rice fritters take some time to make. Selma didn't know what they were having, and merely asked as she came into the hall whether dinner was ready. There was no suggestion of reproach. On the contrary, she offered to fry the rice, so that Alvilde needn't stand about any longer. But even this offended her sister.

However, Selma laid the table. Alvilde had set the fish on the stove. She had the coffee on one gas burner and the fritters on the other. And because of the aroma of frying, she had not smelled that the fish was burning. It tasted vile, but for Alvilde's sake Selma forced herself to eat a little of it; she couldn't manage it all. But she didn't say a word; it was Alvilde who began:

"Yes, I know it's uneatable. You've got every reason to be annoyed. You've a right to expect decent food and to have it ready on time, when I'm living here on charity."

"Oh, now, my dear Villa, I know perfectly well you couldn't help it."

"I admit I can't cook. But there you are—I've never learned. I've always had a maid. And it's no easy matter to learn, let me tell you, when one hasn't the smallest bit of help and has to look twice at every penny."

"My dear, I've no complaints at all. I think you do very well."

"I know I'm sponging on you. But it's not much

4 I

fun for me either, remember. I assure you I ask noth-ing better than to find work and stop being a burden to you."

"Alvilde, you mustn't talk like that. I'm only too glad to be able to help a little."

"And anyway," Alvilde went on, ignoring her, "whether one can do things or not makes no differ-ence when one's *got* to do them. I think I shall have to go down to the Labor Exchange; I'm sure I could find some scrubbing or office-cleaning to do. Think of all the working women who have to do scrubbing and washing, even when they're expecting a child. One shouldn't fancy oneself above such things. Or I could start a soap business, as that friend of yours, Miss Horn, suggested. Me, in a soap shop! Huh!"

"Villa, my darling, don't!" wailed Selma, and tried to hug her. But Alvilde brushed her aside and stood up.

"Well, I expect it'll all be over soon, anyhow. Let's hope I die—I feel so wretchedly ill these days. I re-ally hope I don't get over it—and I hope the baby dies too, so it doesn't have to be dependent on anybody. If it lives, just put it in the workhouse."

"Alvilde!" Selma shrieked. But Alvilde rolled into the bedroom and locked the door. She wept and screamed in there, and though Selma knocked and rattled the door-handle, there was no response.

After Selma had washed up, she came and knocked

on the door again, and at last her sister opened it. She had loosened her clothes, and now dropped straight back onto the bed, where she lay with closed eyes, groaning. Selma sat on the edge of the bed and stroked the other's cheek and hands.

"Villa, dear, are you ill?"

"No," moaned her sister. "Can't you leave me in peace? I've got a headache, and I'm tired."

"What about going out for a little?" Selma suggested tentatively. "Don't you think it's bad for you never to have any exercise or fresh air?"

"Exercise! All very well for you to talk. If you only knew what it was like—"

"Yes, but I've always heard what a bad thing it is to sit indoors the whole time, as you do. We could take it quite slowly—just a little walk up to Sankthans Hill —and then into a teashop," Selma tempted her.

"I can't. You must go alone."

"Of course not. If you don't want to go, I'll stay with you, naturally."

"No, no—you run along. You mustn't make unnecessary sacrifices for my sake. You want to go, obviously."

"Only on your account, my dear."

"Oh, do go—then I can get some sleep. Don't you see I can't sleep when I know you're sitting here—on guard?"

• • •

Up on Sankthans Hill, Selma sat on a bench for a long time. It was wonderfully warm and sunny.

The lawns were rich and green, the trees still in full leaf, yellow and red; the pool reflected their brilliant foliage, the blue sky, and the white clouds. Now and then a yellow leaf drifted down onto the water, while ducks and swans drew ripples across its shining surface.

There were hardly any people up there. At everlonger intervals Selma wiped her eyes with her soaking handkerchief, and simply let the tears flow, oblivious of everything, until someone pushing a pram stopped just behind her and greeted her.

It was Mrs. Gundersen. She sat down beside Selma on the bench and pretended not to notice that the other had been crying. She straightened the covers and kept her eyes on the pram as she rocked it gently and talked about the wonderful weather they'd been having, although it was the middle of October; and she asked for news of the office.

Selma collected herself by degrees and for politeness's sake asked to peep at the baby.

"Well, of course, we think she's lovely. But nobody else would see anything special about her," Beate said deprecatingly as she drew the rug away from the baby's face.

And Selma, in her grief, saw the younger woman's

4 4

smile and the way she stroked the child's cheek, as if the fleeting touch were a delight. And she said: "Fancy daring to bring such a tiny baby out! There's quite a nip in the air. But of course—" and one could hear by her tone that she meant to sound spiteful "—she's not so very tiny. It's some time now since she was born."

Beate merely smiled as before. Selma noticed with a certain satisfaction that Mrs. Gundersen was no longer what she had been. She was quite plump now, and wifely and staid, and it made her look a good deal older.

"Yes, she'll be ten weeks on Monday. I take her out every day when it's fine. She's used to the fresh air, you see. Stener had her out on the balcony before she was a week old."

"What a lot of changes this year has brought you! I must say it's all been very quick," Selma remarked, trying again.

But Beate just smiled.

"Yes, you're right. But I must be getting home now. I always like to have her indoors before the sun sets. Do come along too, Miss Brøter, and we'll have some tea. I baked some oatcakes yesterday, and they're lovely. There's apple jelly, too."

Selma explained that she couldn't come because of her sister; but Beate reassured her. It would do the sister good to sleep. And as she walked beside Beate up Ullevolds Road, Selma began confiding all her sorrows to her.

Beate comforted her. She had heard that many women became quite unreasonable when they were pregnant. It would pass. Selma assured her that Alvilde was very sweet and kind by nature, and normally had a good, even temper—and such a sense of humor! So as soon as all this was over, they'd have good times together again. And of course there would be no difficulty in finding piano pupils. With this Beate agreed.

Selma was thoroughly cheered by the time they reached the Gundersens' gateway. She felt she must help Beate to carry the pram upstairs, and then that she might as well stay for tea. It tasted so good, and it was so pleasant there that she stayed for some time; Gundersen came in just as she was leaving. They both begged her to look in again and bring her sister.

She had a terribly guilty conscience as she raced home, but luckily Alvilde was still asleep and did not wake until Selma had laid the table for supper. And then she was so gentle and amenable that Selma felt really happy.

They saw hardly any people. At first Miss Horn called fairly often, but when she found that Mrs. Dahl absolutely refused to consider any of her plans for starting a business, and preferred to draw her twenty-seven crowns a month, she lost all interest in the Selma-Alvilde ménage. Selma didn't mind much, for Alvilde had never liked Miss Horn.

Møller looked her up now and again. But Alvilde didn't like him either. And one day they received two cards: Kristoffer Møller *cand. pharm.* and Mrs. Daisy Møller. Her maiden name was not given, but one day in the office Miss Brøter met one of the ladies from the pension, who told her that Mrs. Daisy Møller couldn't be said to be *née* at all. Before she became Mrs. Møller, she had kept a tobacconist's shop in Torv Street and called herself Mrs. Rosengrehn. She was also known by the name of Sunset Glow.

But Selma didn't know this when the cards came. She sat looking at them.

"I *am* glad about it!"

"Whatever kind of person can it be who'd take that awful old Møller?" said Alvilde.

"There's a lot of good in Møller," Selma said warmly. "He's no beauty and he's pretty rough, but all the same—I'm very glad. I've really felt sorry for him sometimes, and guilty too. Because I must tell you that he was very keen on me at one time."

"What a fool you were not to take him," said Alvilde. "He's got a bit of money, I know, and if you liked him—"

4 7

"Good heavens, not in that way! Don't be absurd. You surely don't imagine I was the least bit in love with him."

"In love!" snorted Alvilde. "At your age? You ought to have been thankful to get him. At least it would have been better than moldering away as an old maid."

"Certainly not. I'd never marry just for the sake of being married. Ugh, it would be like selling oneself. No, one oughtn't to marry without love; that's my opinion."

"Listen to you! You talk as if you were fifteen instead of thirty-five," her sister said from the rocking-chair. "But, of course, if you think you lead such a gay life already—"

"I prefer it to marrying a man I don't love," answered Selma. "Besides—" and she lowered her voice. "There was someone else I was fond of, so . . ."

Alvilde made no remark, but Selma continued: "That's how it was, you see."

"Why didn't anything come of it, then?" her sister asked after a pause, but quite without interest. "I suppose he didn't care about you?"

"Oh, yes, he did. I'm sure of that—I mean I know it for certain."

"Did he propose, then, or say anything?"

"One knows that sort of thing without having to be told." Selma smiled up at the lamp. "He showed he

was fond of me in lots of ways. He had a way of looking at me when we were out together—yes, how well
I remember that. And he thought of so many things
to please me, and he was always so kind and considerate. We had a lovely time together, the two of us."

"Then why didn't you marry him?"

"Well, it's a long story." Selma sighed. "He was
someone in our office, you see. And there was another
girl there; we used to go out with her, and she made
up to him like anything. Well, that's how it went, and
in the end he was obliged to marry her."

Alvilde rocked herself in the rocking-chair, sitting
with her knees apart and her arms folded over her
stomach, the picture of indifference.

"I don't blame him for anything," Selma said softly.
"She made up to him terribly, as I said; and when a
woman doesn't care what means she uses, well . . .
Men don't always find it easy to resist, you know, especially anyone as innocent and shy as he is. You know,
there was something positively childlike about him. I
could see perfectly well how he felt about me, but he
found it so difficult to put into words—poor man, he
was really embarrassed. And I couldn't bring myself
to encourage him beyond a certain point, you know."

"Oof, yes—men!" said Alvilde.

"But I knew it was I he really loved," Selma continued. "Though as a matter of fact I believe he gets
on quite well with his wife. And they have this baby,

which is a bond between them. And I must say I believe she's become quite capable now, poor little thing, and does her very best to make him comfortable and so on. There's a great deal of good in her, really."

As Alvilde asked no questions, Selma came out with it unurged: "I might just as well tell you. It was Mr. Gundersen. Poor man, even now he'd like to see more of me than he does, and he often asks me to go up there. At first I couldn't face it, but now I think I will look in now and again. If it would give him any pleasure there's nothing I'd rather do."

Afterward in the evenings Selma often tried to return to the subject, but Alvilde made it very plain that she was not interested in Selma's love story. All Alvilde wanted to talk about was her own misfortunes, and especially her pregnancy. Every sensation and discomfort connected with this she described in detail. Time after time she told Selma about the ghastly sufferings she had endured two years before when she had had a stillborn child, and how she was dreading going through it all again.

Selma was in fact intensely interested. With her genuine sympathy was mingled a certain horrified fascination. She began asking questions where her knowledge was at fault, and Alvilde gladly enlightened her.

But how any woman could endure such a thing was more than she could understand. On the November night when she took her sister to the hospital in a car, she trembled as she trudged home afterward, still hearing Alvilde's anguished moans; and she prayed as hard as she could that God might help her.

She didn't undress at all that night. She sat shivering in her solitude, for the stove had gone out and she hadn't the heart to light it again and sit by it in comfort while Alvilde was suffering. What if she never came back—perhaps at this very moment she was dying—O Lord God, help her—!

When she called at the hospital next day, she learned that Alvilde had had a fine boy at two o'clock that morning, and that everything had gone as smoothly and easily as possible. At noon she was allowed to see Alvilde for a moment, lying there so pale and tired and pretty, and peep at the funny little red face—of her nephew!

She hurried home, quite beside herself with joy. Those two little rooms of theirs—she would have liked to start preparing them at once. For the moment that must wait—but how marvelous it would be when Alvilde brought the boy home, and how gay and pretty she would make the place for them. When Alvilde came home—well and lovely and sweet-tempered and merry, as in the old days. And the little boy —oh, the very thought of him! Surely Alvilde would let her help with him now and then—let him be a little bit Aunt Selma's boy, too.

6

MISS BRØTER was sitting with Beate in the Gundersens' bedroom, watching little Beate being put to bed.

It was a sunshiny Saturday afternoon in May. Selma had looked in at the Gundersens' several times that spring.

Beate took the baby from her breast and buttoned her blouse. The baby in her lap was wrapped only in a blanket, which she kept kicking off so as to wriggle and stretch quite naked and free.

Selma bent forward and tickled her under the chin. "Tickle-tickle! Who's a sweetie! She *is* good, Mrs. Gundersen. But I do think she's thin."

"She's been putting on weight quite normally. She never was fat."

"You should see my little nephew now! So plump and sturdy it's a joy to look at him. Deep creases at his wrists and ankles, and dimples everywhere—oh, he's beautiful. Are you sure she's getting enough food? She's over eight months now; oughtn't you to be giving her something besides the breast? You'd soon see how chubby she'd get. Peep-bo! Let's see those fine toofy-pegs, then, baby!"

"She does have other food. I give her oatmeal gruel and boiled egg too. But she still won't eat properly from a spoon—she pats at it and tries to play with it." Beate turned the baby over.

"Oh, yes, our little boy's such a rascal too. Aren't they wonderful to watch just when they've thought out a new trick? The things that boy gets up to you wouldn't believe. You must come along one evening and see him in his bath—I really think that's when they're sweetest. How he kicks and splashes! Your Tulla is much quieter. Do come one evening. You've finished with her by seven. Get your husband to sit with her for an hour or two. Or come on Saturday afternoon, and bring her along."

"Doesn't it make it rather late for the boy, if he's not put to bed until you come home from the office?" asked Beate.

"Oh, he just sleeps longer in the mornings, that's all. And if Alvilde did see to him, it wouldn't be much earlier than that: she has the house to do, and her pupils."

"Couldn't she bathe him in the mornings?"

"She has such a lot to do then. Besides, the boy seems to like it best when I look after him; he screams so when Villa does it—she's quite jealous of me sometimes. Perhaps it's because I have him so often at night."

Beate stood up and laid her baby in the pram.

5 3

"But isn't it rather much for you to have him at night, when you have to get to the office punctually every morning? And the baby's restless, you say. You ought at least to get him into the habit of having his bottle at fixed hours."

"Oh no, our little man would never have that! He screams till he gets what he wants. He's headstrong, for all he's so tiny. And Alvilde can hear him from her room, and feels sorry for him. When she has him she gives him his bottle as soon as he makes a sound. Well, it's understandable: a mother hasn't the heart to let her child cry. Besides, Alvilde's so nervy—naturally. Music lessons are very trying to the nerves, especially for such a genuinely musical person as Alvilde—having to plod along with children and beginners . . ."

"Has your sister many pupils, then?" asked Beate, as they went into the sitting-room.

"Yes, she has four already. That's twenty crowns a month. The only trouble is that they pay so irregularly. Still, they do pay; they're all comfortably off. And we hope she'll get more—she does so want to have plenty to do, poor thing, being so energetic and hard-working. . . ."

Beate fetched a decanter and some glasses from the corner cupboard.

"My cousin in Kragerø sent me some cassis the other day."

"How lovely. Thank you very much. I must be getting along soon, though. Alvilde's going to a concert
this evening; one of her friends invited her. What a
delicious liqueur—such a delicate flavor. I think I
shall try to make some liqueur this autumn. I can't
tell you how wonderful it is to have got a home of my
own again, Mrs. Gundersen. Very different from the
pension. I expect your husband feels the same."

Gundersen let himself in at the front door.

"Here you are, just when Miss Brøter's going," said
Beate when he came in.

"Good evening, Miss Brøter. No, do stay for a moment. We'll have a little sensible conversation for
once. I expect you've been talking nothing but babies up to now," he said, pouring himself a liqueur
and filling Selma's glass.

"No, thank you, no more for me. I must be getting
home. What marvelous weather we're having! Tomorrow I think I'll take my nephew out. Bring your
baby up to Sankthans Hill too, Mrs. Gundersen—it's
so delightful there now. What am I doing, sitting here.
I really *must* go—"

Gundersen brought her coat and held it for her.

"Oh, I *must* tell you. Last time I came here—it was
exactly four weeks ago, and much darker than it is
now. Well, not dark, of course, but dusk. I was going
home along Ullevolds Road when what do you think?
A man came up to me—quite a nice-looking, well-

5 5

dressed young man—charming, really—and said good
evening. Did you ever hear such impudence? 'Fancy
you being on your own this lovely evening,' he said.
'Mayn't I walk with you?' Of course I pretended not
to see or hear him. But just fancy, he walked along
beside me and talked, all the way from the corner of
Sofie Street to Bolteløkken Avenue. Then I caught
sight of a policeman, and I turned and looked the
man straight in the face and said: 'You will please either go this minute, or accompany me to the police
officer over there.' And what do you suppose he did?
He raised his hat and said: 'I'm sorry that such a
pretty girl should be so disagreeable. *Au revoir.*' Then
he melted away—but, you know, I couldn't help
laughing, although my knees were trembling. In fact,
I was still shaking long after I got home."

Gundersen had fetched his hat.

"My dear Mr. Gundersen, you mustn't think of
coming with me."

"Of course I shall. Suppose your unknown adorer
is cruising about after you now, in Ullevolds Road."

"Ugh, yes, that's true. I must confess it's nice to
have company. There's a rather lonely stretch up
there. But I do think it's absurd that a woman can't
be left in peace in the street. Down near the office it's
awful too, you know. I'm always being spoken to.
The other evening in Stener Street somebody actu-

ally put his arm round my waist—a real scallywag from the old town.

"Good-by, Mrs. Gundersen. Thank you very much for this evening. Seriously, do come along one evening and see my boy. I never go home without looking forward to seeing him again and giving him a good hug and a kiss."

Beate had laid supper when Stener got back. She was standing by the balcony door, staring out at the last, pale yellow glow over the houses opposite.

He came and put his arm round her waist, pressing his face into her breast. Beate stroked his hair and neck lingeringly, tenderly.

"It's lovely," she said softly.

He looked up. "Yes." And catching her hand, he put it to his lips.

"I mean that she should be so fond of that baby."

"Oh. Selma Brøter."

Beate nodded. And as if in response to unspoken thoughts, she suddenly threw her arms round his neck and kissed him hard.

But immediately afterward she pushed him gently away. She drew the curtains, lit the lamp, and poured boiling water into the teapot.

"Isn't it odd, though, that we should feel like that? We never know how they're going to turn out. We do know how terrible life can be. And yet it's infinite happiness to have them—children, I mean. What could be more selfish!"

But she smiled as she said it. She turned her head toward the bedroom door, listening, her arm outstretched, arrested in the act of taking something from the table. Stener thought how enchanting she looked, standing at the end of the table with her head bent and that happy smile on her face, her round arm golden in the lamplight.

No sound came from the bedroom; the child was peacefully asleep. Beate handed Stener his cup and sat down.

"I wonder whether she was ever in love," he said.

"Oh, she must have been. When she was young."

"I suppose so. I suppose you all fall in love a little, round about eighteen or twenty."

"I'd never been in love before I met you," said Beate gravely. "And I was nearly twenty-three then. I thought I couldn't—that I was much too old."

Stener took her hand and kissed it.

"Oh, Beate . . . But—" and he stared thoughtfully. "It's a shame about her. She's such a good sort of person. She ought to have had home and children of her own. Now I suppose she'll wear herself out over her sister's baby. And all she'll ever know of lovemaking will be some fellow or other talking to her in the street. And in a way she looks on that as a compliment."

"Yes," said Beate gravely. "But it's a good thing, Stener. Even if a prowler speaks to her or frightens her, she gets a thrill out of it. And when that sister of hers tries to unload as much of the trouble onto her as she can—broken nights, and so on—it makes her happier than she's ever been in her whole life."

"Yes." Stener nodded, smiling slightly. "Perhaps that's what's meant by 'all things work together for good to them that love God.' "

"Yes, perhaps so," said Beate, as gravely as before.

THJODOLF

 *"Sound, healthy 6-weeks baby boy of cultured parents offered to childless couple in comfortable circumstances, to bring up as their own. One definitive payment. Write Box: . . . 'Conscientious.' "*

"It's not easy for me to keep him here, you see," said Miss Erdahl, passing two bent, skinny fingers over her yellow little old face. She looked down at the sleeping baby in its improvised cot of two armchairs pushed together.

The visitor made no reply; she just breathed out as if the heat of the room oppressed her.

It was stiflingly hot in there, and rather dark. The frosty fog hung thick in the courtyard outside, and in the building at the back the windows showed merely as little dark patches. The room was very small. Piles of sewing lay on the table in the window by the sewing-machine, as well as on the round, spindle-legged table under the hanging lamp and on the shabby divan bed along the wall.

6 3

"No, it's not at all easy." Miss Erdahl sighed. "It's wretched pay working for these shops—and then you have to have a fire all day and keep yourself in food and the place clean and all that. I never used to do dressmaking at home like this, you know; unless it might be a bit of work now and then for the people in the other flats here and so on—in the evenings, or in the summer when my employers were in the country. I've got my regulars, you might say, like the Hansens in Underhaugs Road: I've been doing their sewing now for twenty-five years—twenty-five years last April it was. And it takes a lot of time looking after such a tiny mite, doesn't it, what with the feeding-bottles to clean and the washing and all that.

"Otherwise I'd like to have kept him. I've got really quite fond of him.

"Small thanks I'd have got for it, though, mark you! Believe me, Mrs. Johansen, I've done my share of helping that brother of mine and his children one time and another. It was me paid for Fanny to go to the commercial school—that's the child's mother—and this is what I get for it.

"Such a nice, pretty girl she was—and then to go off and do that. Well, see for yourself." She took a photograph from the console table and handed it to the visitor.

Mrs. Johansen glanced at it and gave it back to Miss Erdahl without comment.

"What about the father?" she asked. Her voice was low and rather husky. "Can't he pay anything toward it?"

"Who, him?" Miss Erdahl snorted contemptuously. "Him, with a wife and five children? First he told Fanny he was divorced, then he said he was going to be—but he'll take care not to do that, you may be sure. She's got a little soap business in Herslebs Street, you see, so she's the one who keeps him and the children. If he got a divorce he'd have to pay alimony. *Oh*, no. And how Fanny could behave like that with a person she knew nothing about—well, it's a mystery. Though of course he comes of decent enough people—he graduated from high school and all that. I know that's so, because the Stenders where I work sometimes—they knew about him. He's the son of a doctor where Mrs. Stenders comes from, and she knew one of the boys had gone to the bad and that he was here in town touting for advertisers. That was quite true, she told me."

"It's my husband," Mrs. Johansen said, as quietly as before. "I'd gladly take a child for nothing, but my husband says when they get bigger it means expense—and there's plenty of people willing to pay up to a couple of thousand to get them into a good home—decent people, I mean. So he says five hundred would be the least he could take, he says—"

"There was a woman from out Vaker way—she'd

have taken him for three hundred," said Miss Erdahl. "But somehow I didn't care for her physiometry. . . ."

Miss Erdahl glanced at her visitor, not quite knowing what to make of her. Mrs. Johansen was pretty in a way, but her narrow face was very pale and the skin was taut over her cheekbones. The big steel-gray eyes were deep set and the pale, thin-lipped mouth turned down at the corners. When one looked at her closely one noticed quite a few gray strands in her dark-brown hair, which was parted above the white forehead and drawn smoothly back into a large, plaited bun. Otherwise she might have passed for a young girl—of the kind that is never really young.

An orderly sort of person, at any rate; Miss Erdahl could see that. Her clothes were old-fashioned in cut, but of good material and in good condition. She wore a long, narrow coat, and though her muff and stole were out-of-date in style, they were of good fur, the dressmaker noted. The ostrich feather in the little blue hat was fresh and thick, and at her throat, where she had loosened her outer clothes, there was a line of white and an old-fashioned brooch.

These seemed likely to be quiet, pious people, and comfortably off. They had a house of their own, Mrs. Johansen had mentioned. It would be a good thing if she could place Thjodolf with them, poor little mite;

she was very fond of him, but she longed to get all this over and be rid of Fanny and her affairs.

Meanwhile Helene Johansen was hesitating. There was another thing that Julius had told her she must find out: whether the child was quite healthy and wouldn't bring any filthy disease into the house. But she didn't quite like to ask about this.

"He sweats a lot, doesn't he?" was all she said, as she gently passed her hand over the bedclothes.

"They need to be kept warm, you know, these tiny babies," said Miss Erdahl, bending over the child.

The baby opened a pair of big, dark eyes; his face twisted and reddened and he screamed.

"There, there—auntie fetch his bottle then—there, there, sh—sh—"

Helene sat down again and looked at the screaming baby. Presently, with hesitant little movements, she laid her muff, handbag and stole on the table and picked the baby up in unaccustomed hands. He was wet. She wrapped him in the shawl that had lain over him and placed him in her lap. When she turned him over on his face and rocked him, he stopped crying.

"Was that better then, was it?" she whispered. "That better, little man?"

Gently she supported the soft little face with her work-roughened hand.

"Was you Helene's own boy, then—did you like that, eh?"

2

HELENE walked quickly up Vogts Street. She was shivering a little, after sitting so long with her coat on in Miss Erdahl's hot room.

She was deep in her own thoughts, unaware that she sensed as something familiar the gray dampness of the street and the day. An aunt of her mother's had lived in Thorshaugs Street, and that had been almost the only place Helene had had to go to in the days when she had worked in Christiania.

The frosty fog bit rawly at her face, and it was tiring to walk, for the pavement was slippery and uneven. Out in the roadway the snow had been churned up into brown sugar. In the lightlessness of the day, people looked black and bundled up as they stumped toward her; the houses, soaring into the fog, looked even darker and dirtier than they were, and the frosted windows of the shops shone oily yellow, for their lamps were lit, although it was the middle of the day. Without knowing it, Helene took in all the street noises: the tram groaning up the hill, the tinkling of the harness bells as the horses struggled heavily upward over the difficult surface, the cold, hard ring of picks on the sheet-ice of the pavements, and the whining voices of schoolchildren as they swept past her in flocks.

She went into a greengrocer's and bought two wreaths of spruce fir set with little colored everlasting flowers. Dusk was already falling when she reached the cemetery. The side path lost itself in the fog; it lay white, without footprints in the snow, between the two rows of rime-gray birches. The mist stood like a wall before and behind her as she walked. The grave she was making for was the third from the big yellow wooden crate covering the memorial to the Solum children. Helene laid her wreaths on the little white mound and then for a while she remained standing by it—a narrow black line in the fog.

She hadn't seemed to grieve terribly deeply over Tulla then, ten years ago. It had been so odd and strange in the maternity hospital—embarrassing, too. She had hated it there. And when she had gone back to her home in Drøbak, nothing of what she had been through had seemed real any more—she hadn't felt as if she'd had a baby at all. No one down there had seen it, except Julius the first time he came to visit her, and that was the day after, when Helene had been so ill that she couldn't take anything in properly. And when he came the second time, Tulla was dead.

But later, as the years passed and she had no more children . . . Life grew ever quieter and more desolate. For the last few years Julius had worked as engineer aboard a freighter on the fjord. He came home only for a day every week or so. Because of this she had really missed her mother-in-law after her death four years ago, and that was something Helene never had expected to do. Not that there was any harm in the old creature; they had been quite good friends— only she was so affected and silly. How *could* an old woman behave like that! Amanda said she hadn't been exactly a pattern in her young days—she'd been up to all sorts of things, it seemed. But she was very kind, poor old soul. And now Amanda had gone too; she and her husband had moved to Odda. Helene had never liked Amanda much; she used coarse expressions and was silly and affected with Julius. But now Helene missed her friend. Weeks passed without her having to open her mouth except when she went shopping.

She would love to adopt little Thjodolf. Just that particular baby; not some better-class child whose parents would pay two thousand crowns to get rid of him, but this poor little wretch who was in the way where he was. Poor little thing—and how good he was to stop crying when she picked him up. Thjodolf— what a nice name! Helene said it aloud to herself once or twice as she walked back through the cemetery.

If only she could borrow the hundred crowns. Julius need never know. She had earned a certain amount these last years by doing crochet work and

embroidery for people in Drøbak, and she could easily earn much more: get work from shops in Christiania perhaps—embroider names on trousseaux and
do crochet work: that was in fashion now. And she
worked beautifully and quickly. Should she go to
Mrs. Lund and ask her advice? Perhaps the son—he
was an advocate now—would tell her how to set
about raising that loan.

But when she was sitting in the tram on her way
back into town she felt she couldn't talk to the Lunds
about it. She had never asked them for anything in
her life—she had never asked anyone for anything.
Mrs. Lund was kind; she had always tried to treat
Helene well; but it was odd: although they could be
as good as possible to a servant, they never really
thought about what sort of life she was leading, or
how she felt about things. True, Mrs. Lund had sometimes said: "Is anything wrong, Helene? You look so
sad," but she didn't say it in a way to make Helene
feel able to talk to her about things she couldn't even
sort out properly for herself. No, she couldn't go to
Mrs. Lund with this new idea. It was so difficult to explain, too. . . .

For it would be really ungrateful of her to complain. She and Julius were doing well; they had their
own house, and Helene knew that few homes were as
pretty and clean and well-cared-for as hers. Her summer boarders were always saying so. They wanted to

copy her curtains and mats and everything; they praised her house and garden and her housekeeping, and said how charming and comfortable it was there. And her husband—well, she had no right to grumble at him either. Julius was kind, and usually behaved himself when he was at home. He was a bit careless with money, but she always got as much as she needed from him, and sometimes he had brought her really fine presents—especially in the early days. And if he did racket about a bit with his mates now that he was out and away so much—well, one had to remember that a man like that came up against plenty of temptation. And another thing: Amanda had probably been right when she had said that it was stupid of Helene to be so quiet and serious. Julius liked gaiety and fun, and he was the kind who could always find it, too.

Helene suddenly felt that there were tears in her eyes. She rose abruptly and went out onto the platform; at the next stop she got off and walked on into the town.

Yes, it was her own silly fault. She had been so bad at mixing with people; she had always gone about on her own. Her old home down in Smålens was remote —almost forgotten; she had left it at eighteen. Her parents were dead now, and strangers were living there. All her brothers and sisters were in America. An unhappy love affair had driven her to Christiania.

What happened to her is what often happens to a girl who respects herself and thinks herself above some things: the boy found another girl who wasn't above anything at all. . . . In her two first situations she had had a dreadful, dreadful time; it was nothing but drudgery from early morning until late at night, enduring vulgar, senseless abuse and never hearing a kind word. So when she had gone to the widow lady, Mrs. Lund, she had stayed for ten years. Mrs. Lund was kind and just—indeed she was; so they all were, for that matter. You couldn't count poor Miss Lovisa; it was only natural that she should be fretful, with that injury, and Erna was just a little chit of a girl when Helene was there. As soon as Mrs. Lund found that Helene knew nobody in Christiania and never made any friends, she offered her extra money to work at confirmation frocks for the little girls in her free time. Helene enjoyed earning more, and enjoyed hearing Mrs. Lund say: "Oh, what beautiful work, Helene! How clever you are with your hands!" And when she sat all alone in the maid's room in the evenings, she felt deep, quiet joy at the sight of all the fine white things growing beneath her fingers. Often she sat up far too late because she wanted to see what something looked like when it was finished—the embroidery or the lace that she was working on.

It was so quiet, so very quiet, working like that at

night, with no sound but the ticking of the alarm clock, the gentle whisper of the paraffin lamp, and her own breathing. Now and again she had to straighten her back and breathe out; it was like a sigh. She herself didn't know what she was so deeply sad about; it was as if she were yearning for something. Not the sort of thing the other girls she knew were so taken up with; she didn't care about being with them because they teased her and called her stupid and queer. Sometimes she had gone out with them and met their boys, but she was no more cheerful for that. She had been to services and meetings too, and was none the happier. She visited the old people in Thorshaugs Street—and came back so miserable that she could have lain down and cried.

Then came *the* summer. The Lunds went to Drøbak, for Miss Lovisa was to take the baths. They had rented the house of Hermansen the fisherman, just above where she lived now. Helene got to know the old woman first—she always used to sit in the doorway, and when Helene went by, she called to her and asked questions. Then she took to running over, and would stand by the hour talking to Helene through the kitchen window. One evening Helene met Julius. How all the rest came about she never really knew. She met him on her way to fetch the milk or when she was carrying water. And when he came, and smiled, and showed those white teeth in that handsome brown face, saying: "Out walking, then, Miss?" it was as if something was tickling her inside, and she couldn't help smiling. She heard laughter rippling forth in her own voice—she heard herself laughing; yes, she, who couldn't remember when she had last laughed, had to laugh at Julius until many a time her stomach really ached with it. One Sunday afternoon she went sailing with him; there should have been others there too, but they never turned up. There was a fairly fresh wind when they came out on the water and she was frightened; yet she knew that never in her life had she known anything as glorious as that trip. At night she would stand with Julius under the great lime trees; the fjord glimmered white in the summer night, and there was a good smell of leaves and dust and water. When she came back into her room above the brewhouse where she slept and saw what time it was, she was horrified; but she never found it easy to leave him.

Then came the night when he went up with her to her room. And she remembered how he had pleaded, pressing her close to him, bending her over backward, kissing her; she had begged him to release her and go. But then, when for a moment he loosened his hold—just the tiniest bit—her heart sank like lead; she turned cold with dread lest he should leave her, and dared no longer resist.

Next morning she went about with bowed head, in

7 5

deadly fear. She felt that everyone must be able to see by looking at her what had happened. She felt that her shame must be written in her face. But when she took Erna her coffee—Erna always came down too late for breakfast—the half-grown girl looked suddenly into her face: "Why, Helene, what on earth's happened to you? You're beaming all over. Have you come into a fortune, or something?" Helene began to cry as soon as she was back in the kitchen; yet she knew that it was as Erna had said.

She couldn't understand now how that could have been herself, the way she was that summer and autumn; she had seemed utterly unaware of anything but Julius. They went on meeting in Christiania; when he came to her, her conscience troubled her, yet she felt proud and triumphant too. She was beside herself with shame and fear when she found she was going to have a child, and spoke sharply enough to Julius when she told him about it. All the same, she hadn't really meant all she said. It was rather that she wanted to make *him* say something—she didn't know what. Certainly not what he did say, though he offered her marriage at once; to give him his due, he never tried to get out of it. (She should think not— the very idea! She knew very well she was a fine girl, pretty and clever and respectable, with money in the bank.) Yes, poor Julius; he'd made a great fuss of her, and said he'd got himself something really like a wife. But there was something she had expected—she didn't quite know what—and it had never come.

She seemed to be waiting for Mrs. Lund to say something, as well. She kept thinking of how she would answer when Mrs. Lund complained of her having to leave, and asked her how she could do such a thing. Helene would reply that she was only human, or something like that. But Mrs. Lund said nothing about her leaving at an awkward time, nor that she knew why Helene was in such a hurry to get married. She simply said that Johansen was a good-looking man and that Johansen's place looked very nice, and that she only hoped he would know how to appreciate Helene. And the Lunds gave her half a dozen solid silver teaspoons for a wedding present. Yes, Mrs. Lund had treated her very generously on that occasion too—and yet Helene felt almost disappointed over the sermon she had never had and the answer she had never had the chance to bring out.

Then Helene was married; it was just before Christmas. She moved to Drøbak and to a home of her own. She told herself that she was sorry and ashamed that it had come about in this way. Yet all the same . . . There seemed so little for her to do in that small house, after all that work at the Lunds' place. She had time to sit for hours making baby clothes at the sewing-machine she had bought for herself. During the later months of her pregnancy she slept badly.

She sat up late at night or rose early in the coal-black winter mornings. She couldn't use the machine then for fear of disturbing the others, but she sat by the stove doing crochet work or stitching lace to little shirts and coats. In the stillness she heard the familiar ticking of the alarm clock and the whispering of the lamp, and the burning wood crackling in the stove—and there was the new sound of Julius, sleeping heavily over there in the bed; sometimes she heard the old woman snoring up in the attic. From outside, from the night and the darkness, came the mighty noise of the fjord and the waves breaking on the shore. These new things flowed together in her mind with the feeling of her own changed body and new sensations. She tried to think of what lay before her—of the tiny clothes she held in her hands—clothes she would dress a real live baby in—but she couldn't manage it. She could neither dread it nor long for it; her soul was flooded with serenity. She was still, as a healthy woman is when she waits for what no one can imagine beforehand or describe afterward—something unlike all the queer and complex events of every day, and remote from everyday, uneasy, confused feelings; something simple and straightforward, like the miracles of the Lord Himself.

Then the baby came—and went again, before the mother had really grasped the wonder of it; before it had become bound to her daily life by the thousand cares and worries of that life. She returned to her house with empty hands.

That was ten years ago. She had nothing to remember of those ten years but the busyness with which she had tried to fill her empty hands. Scrubbing, big wash, little wash, sewing and embroidery, crocheting and knitting—busyness that was of no particular benefit to anyone. She moved alone about the scrubbed and shining kitchen; the sitting-room, covered and hung with her needlework, was lived in by visitors for a couple of months in summer; the rest of the time it stood empty.

Once she had had an idea of binding Julius to herself with all this activity. But it was now a long time since he had filled her thoughts as she toiled. The notion had slipped from her mind, and she could not bring herself to reason the matter out.

There had been a time when Julius had seemed to her the finest person in the world. She knew very well that she had no right to complain of him. She ought not to complain when she was so well off. It was simply that she had imagined so many foolish things about him and about how their life together would turn out. She tried not to think of this now, for when she did a queer mood came over her, as if she were ashamed of the kind of person she had been then—as if she pitied herself and envied herself.

• • •

She stood outside the garden fence by the little villa at the back of Hegdehaugen. The fog had lifted a little, so that she could see the green light from the lampshade in the sitting-room shining through the window, with the bare lilac bushes in front. It reminded her vaguely of her own sitting-room windows at home, staring like black, blind eyes behind her own bare lilac bushes.

It seemed so queer to be calling on the Lunds now, the more so because their place had become so grand. So quiet, so spacious. In Helene's day, the children had slept on sofas and camp beds in every room, but it was a big flat for just Mrs. Lund and Miss Lovisa. And there were fine new curtains, and new green damask on the furniture instead of the old covers that Mrs. Lund was forever patching and darning. The grown-up married children had given their mother all these things.

Helene suddenly remembered the day when Mrs. Lund had come to see her in the hospital. She remembered how those old blue eyes had been full of tears; she remembered the dry, worn, mother-hand resting on her own, and heard the old lady's voice: "Oh, Helene, I was so dreadfully sorry to hear about it! How sad, how terribly sad that you should lose your little girl!"

A strange, warm wave surged through Helene, and all at once, dimly yet strongly, she was aware that in

that house sat a mother who had toiled, steadfastly
and willingly; who for her children had worn out all
the youth and strength bestowed on her for the living of her life. There she sat, rich with all that she
had given, while her children flocked about her with
their thanks and little presents; now, her work done,
she rested, and waited for the night. But out here
stood Helene; Helene who had toiled ceaselessly because she couldn't help it; who asked no better than
to toil for someone who should be her own heart's
love. Like ice the thought ran through her that she
couldn't stop working and that it warmed and cheered
no one. She and the lady in there—God had made
them in each other's image; yet one was rich and the
other poor. It had nothing to do with rank or condition.

She felt as if her heart would break. She *had* a right
to complain! All these years she had told herself that
she was well off—that she and her man were well-to-
do for people in their position. Her position was the
same as Mrs. Lund's, yet she was poor, poor,
poor. . . .

Helene heard the limping step in the hall; Miss
Lovisa was coming to open the door.

"Why, good evening! How nice to see you. Mamma,
it's Helene—Helene Østreng, isn't it?" Miss Lovisa
limped ahead into the sitting-room.

"Helene! How nice of you to look in on us

again. Now, do take off your things and stay to supper."

Helene murmured that she was staying with a sister-in-law down in Vika and that they kept early hours there, so "thank you very much, but—" She did take off her coat, however.

Once again it seemed somehow unthinkable to talk to Mrs. Lund about Thjodolf. There was a strange gentleman in the inner room, too—Erna's husband— and that embarrassed her. And there was something about Erna herself that made Helene feel ill-at-ease, though Helene was unaware that it was because she knew that Erna was not quite on a level with the other Lunds: that she was a little too condescending to be quite a lady, and a little too smartly dressed to be well dressed.

But Erna only just looked in to say good evening, and then disappeared again into the inner room. Henriette, who was now married to a Doctor Rolstad, came in and out and laid the table for coffee over by the window, near her mother's chair; it was the maid's day off.

"The cakes aren't what they were in your day, Helene, I'm afraid. You mustn't be too critical. I'm too old to do much myself these days, and nobody has ever made *fattigmann* [1] as well as you did."

Mrs. Lund knitted a child's sock, and talked—

[1] Light pastry made with eggs.

talked about housekeeping and her family, and asked Helene about her housekeeping and her husband. Helene had the impression that these people fancied there were only two or three things she could talk about, and that they were making efforts to keep the conversation going on those things. Even Henriette, whom Helene had been so fond of, and who had been such a sweet child . . . No, they could never have imagined what was on her mind; and she wasn't able to turn the conversation her way even when Henriette brought out photographs of her children to show her.

It wasn't until she was on the point of leaving, and the son—who was now a lawyer—was holding her coat for her. . . . Then it was that Erna stuck her head in through the curtains: "I say, Helene—how many rooms have you got—to let in the summer, I mean?"

"We often let the two rooms downstairs, and Mother's old bedroom in the attic."

"The thing is, I was thinking of taking rooms with you this summer, but that would be a bit small—although the children and the girl could sleep in the attic, so that would be— Because then I'd only need to bring one maid; you could give us breakfast and supper, couldn't you, and we'd get dinner at the hotel. What do you think?"

Helene hesitated.

"Well," she said softly, "it's just that I don't know whether I could manage it this year. We've been thinking of taking a foster child—that's what I came to town to see about."

"No, really? Are you going to take in a child?" said Henriette.

"A relative, then, or—?" asked Miss Lovisa.

"Don't you do it, Helene!" said Erna. "You've no *idea* what you're taking on—you've never had any of your own. You just don't know what a trouble it is—and how little they pay foster parents. They do, you know. Oh, Helene, don't."

"Well, you see, it's sort of lonely being on my own so much. And he's such a bonny little boy, the one we're thinking of," said Helene. "Such a good baby—"

Old Mrs. Lund pulled forward a chair.

"Sit down again for a minute, Helene. There's not all that hurry, surely."

And almost before Helene knew it she had told them all about Thjodolf. Mrs. Lund and Henriette were very attentive, and she saw that they understood. Even the money was easy to talk about; and she never mentioned Julius at all. It was obvious that she would need a little cash for expenses at first, and for something in reserve.

"I tell you what, Helene," said Erna, "you can have my pram, if you really are going to take this child. It's as good as new—it just wants touching up with a bit of enamel, and your husband can do that."

"Oh, that's very kind—thank you—but I couldn't accept it."

"Nonsense! It only takes up space where it is."

"But you might need it again—"

"God forbid. I'll take care of that. Two's plenty for *me*, thank you."

To her annoyance, Helene felt herself blushing. She felt the blood mounting to her cheeks for shame at the way the other woman spoke.

Lawyer Lund was thinking how odd it was that he had never noticed the beauty of Helene. Hers was a type one most often met abroad; in France and Italy he had seen nuns with that kind of face: pale and pure, hardened and sensitive at the same time.

He walked down into the town with her.

"Yes, of course; you know I'll help you to borrow from the bank. But how is it you want to leave your husband out of it?"

"Oh—well," said Helene slowly. "I somehow thought it would be right for *me* to pay a little to have the boy—I shall have most pleasure from him, after all."

"Now, listen, Helene. My wife and I give a couple of hundred crowns every year to orphanages and so on—in memory of our little girl who died. But if you'd allow us to give you the money you need—no, no, you know I understand—it couldn't possibly be put to better use for a child. No, you can't refuse—and don't thank me, either. Thjodolf can do that when he's older—after he's thanked you. . . ."

3

THE evening that Helene brought Thjodolf home there was a fresh southwest wind, so that the steamer was delayed.

She had half expected Julius to be on the landing-stage, for it was the time when he was usually at home. But there was no one. She had to put the pram into the shed, for she had wrapped it up. Tired and dizzy after the voyage in the hot, nauseating cabin—Helene was not a good sailor—she set off for home with the basket and the child bundled in shawls in her arms. The ground was wet and icy, and she slipped and slid, for the wind was behind her and it was hard to see where she was going; the lights wavered and flickered as the wind tore at the lamps. The roar of the fjord and the soughing of the wind in the treetops in the gardens filled her ears. Now and then cold thaw-drops fell on her, and she drew the shawl yet closer about the child and began to run a little through the dark, dissolving night.

It was dark at home. The four windows facing the

road were always dark and blind, for they belonged to the two rooms they never used; but whenever there was anyone in, the light from the kitchen window at the gable end shone out onto the bushes. The house was a pretty little white one, standing on a slope; the garden ran right down to the road and ended with a high stone wall.

The slope was like glass, and water was pouring down it. Helene found the key in a hollow of the stone wall where she had put it when she left. And when she had let herself in, she felt the chill, raw air from the dark kitchen coming to meet her. Julius probably hadn't been home at all since she'd gone away.

It was too cold here for the baby; she had to run over with him to Mrs. Hansen and ask her to keep him for the moment.

There were three or four women in the little base-ment shop, and of course they clustered about Helene when she came in with the bundle of shawls and ex-plained that this was her new foster child. They all went into the back room with her and peeped as she unwound the shawls and laid the baby in Mrs. Han-sen's bed. Then they began to ask questions. Helene disliked this; she had always been in the habit of keeping herself to herself. But, "Well, he's a good little fellow," she said, with a smile that was half trou-bled, half proud.

But the women cried: "Bless my soul—eight weeks d'you say he is? Puny for his age, then. Poor mite— looks like rickets to me. One payment, once and for all, eh? Ah, he'll never make old bones—dear me, no, I can see that from his eyes, mark my words."

Helene's face was flushed and her lips were pressed hard together when she came back to her kitchen. She rattled and clattered the rings of the stove and punched the eiderdowns with her fists when she stripped the bed to get the chill out of it. She would have to have Thjodolf in her own bed tonight, as the pram was still down at the landing-stage. She took out the clothes that Miss Erdahl had given her in a basket, and looked at them. Pooh, how badly washed and ironed they were! She threw them all into a pail, with the things he had wetted on the journey, and put the pail outside on the porch.

Her own baby's clothes lay in her mother-in-law's chest of drawers in the attic passage. Helene picked up the lamp and went to fetch them, and brought down her apron full. Little by little her movements became more as they usually were: gentle, quiet, swift but not hasty, as she rearranged the chest of drawers at the foot of her bed, emptied the bottom drawer, and put the baby clothes into it. Now and then she paused to look closely at some especially finely worked gar- ment, with its pretty lace and tucks. Yes, they were well made; they'd said so at the hospital too; she had taken the whole lot in with her, like a silly, not knowing one mustn't use one's own things there. So none of them had ever been worn.

Ah, that was to have been the christening-robe. A pity, really, that Thjodolf had been christened already.

She changed the things round, removing the shirt she had hung out to air with all the rest in front of the stove. He should have his best shirt on, his first night in the house.

Then she took the last feeding-bottle from Miss Erdahl's basket, stood it in a saucepan of water to warm, threw her shawl round her, and ran to fetch Thjodolf.

When she had locked the kitchen door behind her again and stood in her own home with the child, she had a strange feeling; a feeling almost of embarrassment.

"Peep-peep!" She lifted him up toward the lamp. "Going to live here now, was he? Like it here then, did he? Peep-peep." How solemnly he stared at the lamp. He was perfectly good now, and yet he'd bellowed all the time he was over at the shop, Mrs. Hansen said. "Peep-peep!" said Helene softly.

That it should be so difficult to change a baby! Helene felt all thumbs. And then he began to scream and she couldn't make out why; perhaps the washing-water was too cold or too hot; she dipped her hand in over and over again. "Whadda matter den?" she asked, in the same gentle, shy voice, and fiddled with tapes and safety pins. She was drenched right through apron, skirt, and everything by the time she had bathed him.

She stayed there on the stool in front of the stove with the baby on her lap, and fed him. He fell asleep before he had quite finished; Helene laid him carefully in her bed and covered him over.

Then she cut bread for herself and poured out some coffee. Thoughtfully she stared at the lamp while she ate. It was just as well, really, that Julius wasn't at home; he'd only have irritated her.

She washed up the few things, and boiled milk and water for the baby as Miss Erdahl had shown her. Then quietly she undressed.

She'd better leave a light burning tonight, perhaps; she wasn't used to having a child in her bed, and she might crush it. Helene fetched the tiny pale-blue lamp from the stand in the sitting-room, filled it, and stood it in a hand basin of water on a kitchen chair, too far from the bed for her to knock it over in her sleep. Then she put out the kitchen lamp and crept into bed beside the baby.

The little night lamp filled the room with a soft, moon-blue dusk, and threw a big, round, golden splash of light on the white ceiling. Helene lay still and gazed up at it.

Presently she stole an arm round the boy and drew him to her. He was snug and warm and sleeping soundly.

She lay listening to the intermittent roar of the waves on the shore and the wind soughing in the trees. Tonight there was nothing dreadful in it. It was almost cosy to lie and listen to it; it seemed to remind her of something good that had been, once upon a time.

Twice during the night she had to get up, change the baby, and get a bottle for him. But both times she had the odd feeling that she was waking up to something good: it was lovely to lie down again in the blue glimmer of the night lamp and listen to the southwester droning round the house and the fjord waters breaking along the shore.

4

THJODOLF did well. At first he was a little out of sorts, and Helene took him to the doctor, who said that the child was delicate, but that with proper care . . . And proper care he had, especially when spring came and he could be taken out into the fresh air; he picked up then, and throve, so that it was a pleasure to see him. And he was such a pretty child! His light-brown hair formed a big curl above his forehead, and what beautiful eyes he had. . . . "Ah, he's a dood boy, this boy is," Helene told him; but only when there was no one to overhear her. Julius teased her quite enough as it was over this little lad of hers.

All the same, Julius liked having him. He had cleaned up the pram and enameled it until it was as good as new, and on his Sundays at home he liked to go out with Helene when she took the baby for an airing. On weekdays she usually stood Thjodolf's pram under the sunny wall at the corner of the house, where she could see him from the kitchen window, but on Sunday afternoons she liked to take him into the town; for she was proud enough of the pretty, well-cared-for child. None of the grand families there had a finer pram; and there were frills on the pillow-case and insertion work in the sheet, as well as a beautifully crocheted pram rug lined with blue satin. The baby's coat and cap were trimmed with swansdown.

Julius and Helene had really got on better together since they had taken the baby into their home. Helene might wriggle a little and say "Go along with you" when he grabbed at her, but not so crossly as she had done during the past few years. Julius knew very well that she didn't mean much by it, and that in fact she liked it when he caught hold of her and cuddled her. Now when she struggled it was more as if she were fooling with a youngster—and she turned so pink and pretty, Julius said. Remembering the time when they first knew each other, she couldn't rid herself of that strange sore feeling deep within her—they were not like that together now. She knew Julius now; poor fellow, he couldn't help being what he was: a big, stupid boy, for all his forty-four years. But there was a lot of good in old Julius; most women had far worse husbands to put up with. If only they'd had children! He might well have been different then; there would have been more life and fun to come home to. And she was fond of poor old Julius, too.

He had taken charge of Thjodolf's bankbook. There was nothing to be done about that, and it was better not to think of it. So long as Lawyer Lund didn't get to hear of it, things must stay as they were. Helene had another bankbook for the boy, and into that account she paid what she earned by her needle-work. As she worked at her crochet—she was making a bedspread for one of the ladies of the garrison—she amused herself by planning how she would show Thjodolf the book on his confirmation day. After coming home from church and having dinner—she would have roast veal that day, with cream sauce and many different sorts of jelly, followed by a layer cake like the one the Lunds had had for Erna at her confirmation—and after Julius had lain down for his nap, she would take the boy into the sitting-room and show him his bankbook. "This is for you, from your mum, boy," she would say. And she would tell him how she had slaved and scraped it all together for him, ever since he'd lain in his pram. And she'd sit with him, and they would talk quietly—so as not to wake Julius—about what to do with the money. Helene thought he ought to go to the Treider commercial school. She pictured Thjodolf in his confirmation suit as a steady, ambitious young man—something like Mrs. Sahlkvist's Martin, only much better-looking; for Martin wasn't exactly handsome. But he was the kind who got on just by being clever and reliable. Martin was head of a department now, so why not Thjodolf—at the very least?

"Yes, little man," she said, rocking the baby as she took him up to attend to him. "Is you my boy, then—is you Mummy's golden boy?" She pressed him close and smacked his hand against her cheek. "Poor Mummy—poor Mummy, den—"

But when Julius was at home she never talked to the child like that—never called herself Mummy. And once when Julius took Thjodolf on to his knees and butted him with his head, saying: "Ain't you scared of your daddy, then? Bump him, would you, cheeky?" Helene took the boy away from him, saying rather sharply: "Don't act so silly—you know very well he's too young to play games yet, poor little mite!"

She never thought of Julius as Thjodolf's daddy,

and didn't know why she disliked it when he called himself so.

Then came a certain Sunday at the end of June.

Helene was sitting in the sun, at the table by the window. Her arms were folded under her breast and she was reading a Nat Pinkerton paperback; Julius sometimes brought one home with him.

She was enjoying herself. She had done the week's wash; the bedspread and curtain gleamed with whiteness, and she had put on the old blue print dress with the white flowers which she liked so much. The food was ready on the stove, waiting for Julius to come in —for he had gone out with some friends. There was an appetising smell of *lapskaus* [2] and coffee, which blended with the scent of flowers in the garden and the fragrance of the yellow roses in a vase on the table; Helene found the first blooms on the big bush at the end of the house when she put the pram out under the sunny wall a little while before.

Then, as she looked up from her book and out at the road after Julius, she saw a bright-scarlet silk parasol down by the corner. It blazed against the sunwhite water and all the green that was veiled and bleached by dust and sunshine. The parasol was coming up their slope, carried by a lady in a white suit.

[2] A meat-and-vegetable stew.

9 5

Probably it was someone from town coming to ask about a room for the summer, Helene thought. There came a step on the porch, then a knock on the door.

Helene opened it.

"Good morning. Is this where Engineer Johansen lives?"

"Yes, that's right," said Helene.

The lady was young and pretty, fair-haired and plump. The parasol cast a faint rosy glow over her face and the upper half of her figure. She wore a white linen suit, rather short in the skirt, and white stockings and shoes.

For a moment she stood there without speaking, and Helene was on the point of telling her that all her rooms were booked up for the summer. Then the lady said: "Is it you who have a foster child—a little boy called Thjodolf Erdahl? It's—I'm his mother."

Helene said nothing. The other closed her parasol, rested the tip of it on the floor of the porch and twirled the handle between her hands as she said: "I thought I must come down and see him—I have missed him so. I thought I must come down and see how he's getting on."

"Oh, yes. Please come in," said Helene. "Such a state as the place is in—" She tidied the books on the table. The room otherwise was like a new pin.

The stranger looked about her.

"I've got him outside now," said Helene. "I don't

know—most likely he's asleep. He usually sleeps about this time." She went to the door and out, followed by the visitor.

Of course she *had* to come when the baby had on a dirty frock, thought Helene, and everything about him dirty. She hadn't wanted to change him until after dinner, when they were going to the park to listen to the band: that had been the plan. His clean clothes lay freshly ironed on the table in the sitting-room.

"Oh, what a charming garden you have," said the strange lady; and then they reached the pram, which stood on the gravel path where peonies and long-stemmed yellow lilies hung over in a wave from the old bed.

"Oh, how he's grown!" the mother said, and for some time she bent and looked in under the hood at the sleeping baby. "How big he's grown, my little Thjodolf—and how pretty, too!"

The mother wiped her eyes with a little handkerchief as they went in. In the kitchen she sat down in the rocking-hair, dabbed her handkerchief over her face and twisted it in her fingers. Helene sat on the same chair as before.

She wasn't really so pretty, after all. And she had powder on her face—you could see it, now that she'd been crying. She showed her legs almost to the knees, the way she sat—and her feet seemed on the point of bursting out of the white canvas shoes. Under her linen jacket she wore a thin, crumpled white blouse, through which lace underclothes could be seen, with red ribbons strung through them. She didn't look like someone who has learned to be careful after being in trouble.

"How strange it is to see him," she said, looking up at Helene.

"Yes. I expect you notice a change in him since you saw him last."

"I should think so! Poor soul, he was a wretched little thing when he was born. They didn't think he'd live, you know, up at the hospital. And, oh, how ill I was with him—and that time he was with Aunt Lovise—poor thing, she hadn't an idea how to look after a baby. Every time I went and saw him there I thought, that's the last time I shall see *him* alive. And now—!"

"And how like his daddy he is!" The mother's voice shook a little. The childless woman felt something like a stab at her heart. She remained silent.

"Oh, yes—yes—yes," sighed the mother.

Helene looked down and rubbed the palm of her hand to and fro along the edge of the table, as she said: "No, it can't have been easy for your aunt to have the child—she'd hardly know what to do with such a tiny baby, I expect."

"Oh, no, it wasn't easy for her."

They sat quiet for a little.

"You haven't any children of your own, have you? I believe my aunt said—"

"I had a little girl," said Helene quickly. "But she died, and I never had any more." She looked down again.

Then the door opened; it was Julius. He stopped short and looked at the visitor in surprise.

"This is Thjodolf's mother," Helene told him.

"Oh, yes? Good morning to you," said Julius, taking the visitor's outstretched hand.

She had risen, and now said: "And you'll be Thjodolf's foster father."

"Ay, that's about it." Julius laughed a little awkwardly. He was better-looking when he didn't laugh. He was a heavy, big-built fellow, with quick brown eyes and a brown, curly forelock, but he had lost some of his front teeth now.

"Come down to have a look at your boy then, have you?"

"Yes, I thought—now the weather's so fine—" She looked up into his face. "You can't help longing, you know. But now I see what a good place he's come to, and what kind people— " and again she put her handkerchief to her eyes.

"Aha, ay." Julius was embarrassed. "Ay, Thjodolf's the lad, all right," he rambled on. "Not that I know anything about such things, mind you—but there's such a fuss made of him you'd never believe. I get to hear it, you know. The wife—" he jerked his head backwards at Helene "—she's a caution. So he does what he's got to do on what he's got to do it on—ain't that so, Helene?" He laughed aloud and winked at them both.

"Ah, go along with you," said his wife. She was taking plates down from the rack. "We were just going to have our dinner; would you care to—?"

"Well, thank you," said the visitor. "As a matter of fact, I was just going to ask you if there was a restaurant or something—I don't know anyone here, so—"

"An honor, Miss, an honor. Stay and have a bite with us. Helene, I'll just nip over to Mrs. Hansen and get another bottle of beer—" and Julius swung out of the door.

"If you stay you'll be able to see him when he wakes," said Helene, and she put out knives and forks.

Julius was in high good humor during the meal. And Thjodolf's mother—her name was Fanny Erdahl—began to liven up. She chattered away about herself—about how horrid and spiteful the other women had always been when she was in the office of a paper business in Storgaten where she met Thjodolf's father. Now she was cashier at a big butcher's out Grønland way. And here too it seemed she had quarreled with the rest of the staff. Julius doubled up with laughter at her account of the butcher's fat, conceited wife, and of how Fanny wouldn't be spoken to like that and answered back.

It was while they were having coffee that Helene heard the baby crying, and both women ran out to fetch him in.

Fanny Erdahl laughed and wept by turns in delight over her child; she thought he was so sweet. She took him on her lap to give him his oatmeal gruel; for he had begun to eat gruel from a spoon now. And she laughed because he was so greedy and she herself so clumsy; she spilled the food on the table and down the boy's bib. Then suddenly she lifted the child into the air and stared at the mustard-yellow patch that had appeared on the lap of the white suit—she looked in amazement at Helene and Julius and then at the stain again. Helene couldn't help smiling, and Julius laughed and slapped his thighs.

"That's kids for you! You can't never trust 'em, eh? Hee-hee-hee!"

Helene had to feed Thjodolf. Then she changed him and dressed him in the new white smock and linen hat. There were no bounds to his mother's rapture; he was *such* a beautiful boy.

Miss Erdahl went to the park with them and listened to the music. Helene had washed out the mess Thjodolf had made and ironed the skirt dry; and Julius was quite proud to be walking out with the charming lady; for charming she was with her red parasol against the afternoon sun. Her face and the top part of her suit looked quite rosy. She and Julius walked ahead, talking, and Helene followed silently with the pram a step or two behind them.

Helene and Julius went with Fanny to the landing-stage, with Thjodolf in the pram. And she thanked them repeatedly for the pleasant day she had spent with them.

Julius smirked and chuckled all that evening.

"One of the right sort, she was," he kept saying. "No flies on *her*."

"Ugh, I thought she was a proper show-off," said Helene.

"Show-off, d'you call her?" Julius laughed even more. He was sitting on the edge of the bed, pulling off his socks. And he threw his arms round Helene, who was just going to get into bed. "Everybody can't be as prim and proper as you, you know!"

"That's the kind you like—I can see that," said Helene tartly, and she broke away from him, adding as she settled down in the bed: "You'd have liked somebody like that for a wife, I expect."

"For a *wife*? No fear. Not *that* one. I wasn't born yesterday. No, you're the sort to marry."

Helene received his caresses, though she was still a little annoyed with him. And just as she was dropping off to sleep she heard Julius chuckling to himself again: "Ay, by golly, she was one of the right sort, that Miss Erdahl!"

5

FOR Helene the summer passed quietly and peacefully. She had let her rooms to two elderly single ladies from Christiania, who cooked their own meals on a primus stove and needed no waiting on, so that she had leisure to sit for long spells in the porch and work at the curtains that Erna had ordered. She had made an excuse not to let her rooms to Erna—somehow she didn't feel like having people she knew on top of her—and Erna had rented a house farther along toward Husvik. Sometimes her nursemaid looked in on Helene when she was out walking with the two little girls; she was a pleasant, quiet, elderly person, and the children were really very good. The elder one loved to push Thjodolf in his pram to and fro in front of the porch. They were well-brought-up, and thanked Helene very prettily when she gave each of them a plate of berries from the garden. One Sunday Henriette came too; she was staying with her sister. She had coffee with Helene and was very friendly; she said that Thjodolf was an exceptionally pretty baby and that he had an unusual amount of hair for his age. None of hers had had nearly as much.

Julius was now working on a boat that made shorter trips, so that during that summer he was more often at home. Not that he stayed about the house much when he was ashore; he went out with his mates and was quite often a little fuddled when he came home. He wasn't as easy to get money out of, either, as he had been, and once or twice Helene had to be really cross with him over it.

But in general she took her husband's failings fairly lightly now. Julius was a kind fellow at heart and did his best to behave himself at home, even when he'd had a skinful. On the whole they got on pleasantly enough together, and Julius was helpful and handy about the house. He would bring back freshly caught fish which Helene cooked and served with parsley butter and crisp-bread spread thick with farm butter, and new potatoes from the garden; and with it went a half-bottle of beer and a big nip for Julius. Helene would allow no spirits in the house except for the bottle of aqua vitae she herself bought and kept locked up in the cupboard. She poured out a generous dram for his dinner, and that was that. He submitted to this and never tried to drink any more at home; she'd broken him of that.

Only once was there trouble. It was a Sunday early in September, and that woman Fanny Erdahl came to see Thjodolf. Helene had looked forward to a really nice day; Julius had been out that night and brought back a fine cod, and during the week he had picked raspberries for her. She made jelly of them, and with the remains had prepared an extra special dish of raspberry fool, which they were to have for dinner. Then that Fanny arrived, early in the morning when Julius was still in bed. Helene stayed with her at the bottom of the garden while he got up, and then it somehow came about that Julius took Fanny for a walk up to Seiersten while Helene tidied the house and got the dinner.

When they sat down at the table, Julius jokingly offered the lady a dram, which she accepted. So Helene had to leave the bottle on the table. Julius took full advantage of this, and Fanny herself wasn't backward either. Helene couldn't make her out. At first she had thought that Fanny claimed to be a lady and fancied herself a cut above them. Not that having a child by a married man was particularly ladylike; but her father had been a primary-school master and she must have had some sort of upbringing. Yet there she sat swallowing drink after drink, saying *skål* and simpering and playing up to Julius—oh, well, she must just be made like that, the hussy, and couldn't help showing off to every man she saw.

After dinner the others took it into their heads to go for a row in the fine weather. Helene couldn't go with them; she dared not take Thjodolf out on the water, for he had a cold and was a little out of sorts anyway as he was teething. Miss Erdahl did say something about Helene finding someone to sit with him for a little, but she could hear from her tone of voice that they weren't keen on having her with them. So off they went, the two of them, while Helene sat at home with the baby, who was whiny and whimpery and snively and sore-skinned too. She rocked and soothed him in her lap and walked up and down the kitchen crooning to him. And now and then she pressed his little face to her cheek: "Thjodolf's *my* boy, isn't he? My own little boy, he is—mine."

Why that woman kept haunting the place was more than Helene could understand. After all, she had given the boy away. And when she did come, she barely glanced at him; she wanted to bathe—go for a walk—pick flowers. But no doubt she liked having a place to go to on Sundays.

Once Fanny mentioned that her aunt wanted very much to come out with her one day to see Thjodolf. Helene said yes, certainly, it would be very nice if old Miss Erdahl would come. And she bought a joint of meat for the day she expected them; she wanted to have everything especially nice for the old soul: it probably wasn't often she got out anywhere. And then Fanny went and brought a friend instead, saying she hoped Mrs. Johansen didn't mind, but that she *had* said she might bring somebody. And the friend was another of the same sort.

It was dreadful. Poor Thjodolf, having that mother to be ashamed of when he grew up. For if Fanny didn't go properly off the rails sooner or later—well, it would be a marvel, thought Helene.

"But never you bother your head about that, Toddie," she said to the baby in the pram. "You're my boy, see, and Helene's your mum—isn't she, my precious?"

But the last time that Fanny Erdahl came down to see the child, Helene felt really sorry for her. It was at the end of November and the weather was frightful, but Fanny had on a gray check suit of some sort of thin stuff with hardly any wool in it; an old spring suit probably, out-of-date in style, and dirty, with several buttons missing. Under it she wore a miserable little crocheted cardigan and a stained, bright-red, satiny blouse of some thin, sleazy material. She was soaked through, and Helene had to lend her a change of clothes; and when she hung Fanny's things out to dry, she noticed that her boots were split and her stockings full of holes.

Julius wasn't at home that day, so Helene hadn't meant to cook any dinner. But she brewed some strong coffee and boiled some eggs and spread wheatcakes with goat's cheese, and Fanny ate as if she hadn't seen food for days. Tears kept coming into her eyes, too, but at first she didn't say much. She asked if she

might give Thjodolf his egg, but he had begun to be
shy of strangers, and screamed when his mother tried
to take him, so that Helene had to set him on her own
lap. He sat there fairly contentedly, smearing himself
with his wheatcake, and his mother sat and gazed at
him while her tears dripped and dripped. Helene
was sorry for the woman and said: "They're all like
that for a time, you know—shy of strangers. When
he gets older, and remembers you from one time to
the next, like—"

The mother burst into loud weeping.

"I just don't know when the next time will be!

"I've lost my job now," she went on presently.
"And it won't be easy for me to get another. I daren't
show myself to anybody even—I've no clothes or anything."

Little by little it all came out. She had lost her position because her accounts were wrong, and the
butcher's wife had vowed that wherever Fanny went
next her employers should know what kind of person she was. She was wild because her husband had
liked Fanny—as if Fanny could help that! Ugh, he
was a disgusting old beast; often he'd taken such liberties with her that she felt quite sick; he was an old
pig. But she hadn't dared to choke him off too
sharply, or she'd have been sacked for that. And the
old hag had been up telling tales to Aunt Lovise, giving her *her* version, and Aunt Lovise was so furious

that Fanny would never dare show her face there again. Now she was staying with a girl—a friend of hers—who rented a maid's room up in Neuberg Street, but she couldn't stop there for long because Selma herself wasn't too well off, poor thing. If only Fanny could have got a bit of sewing to do; Selma had a sewing-machine.

Helene wanted to comfort the poor woman, but it wasn't easy to find anything to say. So she made more coffee and did some sewing, letting the other talk until she grew calmer. And bit by bit Fanny's mood brightened. Thjodolf became used to the strange face and was no longer afraid; Helene picked him up and made him show off his few little tricks: pat-a-cake pat-a-cake, butt-a-billy-goat, and peep-bo through his fingers. He was over eleven months old now, and had six teeth, and he crawled about when Helene put him down on the floor. He was very sweet, and often so funny that you could die laughing.

Outside, the rain and sleet poured down, so they stayed cosily indoors. Fanny took Thjodolf on to her lap, and he was gentle and sweet; he played with the buttons of her blouse and tried to bite them, and when she poked him under the chin and said "tickle-tickle!" he laughed till he nearly choked.

Helene asked Fanny to stay the night, thinking it would be so miserable for her to set out in that awful weather and not get back to town until late at night—

and then to trudge wet and wretched and alone back to the friend's room in Neuberg Street. So Helene got supper and bathed Thjodolf, though he had had a bath the evening before, so that his mother might watch him splashing in the basin. And Fanny laid the fresh, clean, sweet baby in the pram and sat and rocked him until he fell asleep.

"Oh dear, oh dear!" she said, and wept again. "If only I could have kept him myself. Surely you must understand—if a stranger like you can be so fond of him, what must I feel—his own mother!"

The winter went on and Helene heard no more from Thjodolf's mother—not even on the boy's birthday or at Christmas; she didn't even know her present address.

In March, Julius took a job as engineer at a factory in Christiania. He talked of selling the Drøbak place, so that they could move into town for good; but there was a housing shortage there now, so for the time being Julius was to share a room with a fellow workman and Helene stay on in Drøbak. He went out there on Sundays, but not every Sunday.

Helene didn't mind very much. She only hoped this arrangement might last, though it meant that she would see even less of her husband than before, for she dreaded having to move to the town. For one thing, she was afraid that if she did, Fanny Erdahl would be continually on her doorstep. But apart from that, she had grown very fond of her home and her garden, and marveled that Julius could bear to think of leaving.

The child was now such fun and such good company that she wished for nothing more. He was a little puny, poor little soul, certainly; he had a touch of rickets and caught cold easily, so that she had been afraid of bronchitis and had taken him to the doctor twice. But thank goodness it had been no more than an ordinary chill.

"He's not very strong," the doctor said. "But with all the good care you take of him, Mrs. Johansen, he'll grow up fine and sturdy yet; there's nothing there to worry about."

And when spring came, for the second time in Thjodolf's life, he could call "Mummy!" and say "b'ead" and "seeze" when Helene put bread and cheese on the table; and when she went her errands, carrying him on her arm, he pointed to all the animals they met and said "pussy." In the shops she set him down on the floor, for he could stand now if he held onto her skirt. Helene was very proud of her boy. He wasn't as chubby as some, but the doctor said it wasn't a good thing for babies to be too fat—and there wasn't a child in the whole town with such beautiful brown curly hair as little Thjodolf had.

There were big, yellowish buds on the bushes in

the garden, and the spiraea hedge was a tender, luminous green. Swallows flashed round the house in lightning sweeps and darted with chirps and twitters in and out of their nests under the eaves.

Helene walked along the flower bed in front of the house and saw how big the auricula buds were, and how the daffodils were coming along. She carried the child on her arm and put him down on the sun-warmed gravel of the path; then she ran three or four steps away from him, and crouched. The child stood for a moment, made a face as if he were going to cry, sagged at the knees and stretched his arms out to Helene. Then all at once he plucked up courage, and with a little squeak like the swallows' he staggered the few steps to the mother and fell into her outstretched arms.

Helen rejoiced and pressed him to her, and the tiny boy rejoiced too, delighted with his own achievement. They did it again and again, and Thjodolf grew more and more enraptured with the new game.

In another six weeks, when the yellow rose bushes were in full bloom, Helene could sit on the lawn with her sewing and keep an eye on Thjodolf as he staggered about fairly briskly, playing with a big wooden horse that Julius had brought back from town. Helene had named it Jakob after a horse they had had at her old home when she was small, but Thjodolf called it Lakel.

6

ONE weekday in July when Helene was ironing, the kitchen door opened behind her and Fanny Erdahl walked in.

She was beaming all over her face and was as changed as could be: gay and pretty, smartly and stylishly dressed in a tailor-made suit of gabardine, high brown boots of the kind that had buckles high up round the calf, and a pale-blue hat of net on her golden-yellow hair.

"Busy as ever!" she cried in greeting; and Helene noticed that her tone was quite different from what it had ever been before. It was protecting—almost patronizing.

"And there's my Toddie! There's my darling boy. How fine and big you've grown—come along to this mummy, then; let me look at you. Give Mummy a kiss."

Thjodolf was no longer frightened of strangers, and he came fairly readily; but when his mother went on kissing and kissing him he grunted a little and pushed away her face with his little hands. Then, seeing the chocolate and the big teddy bear she had brought him, he settled down quite contentedly in her lap.

Helene folded the ironing-cloth, set the iron at the back of the stove, and cleared away the clothes. Then she put on the coffeepot.

"Ah, coffee!" said Fanny Erdahl. "How lovely that'll be. And, oh, how happy I am to be sitting here again—how I've longed for this!" Her eyes sparkled with delight as she looked into Helene's face.

"You'll never guess what great news I have for you this time," she said, as Helene poured out the coffee and put down the Vienna bread that she had fetched. Fanny Erdahl paused for a moment. "I'm going to— I've got married!" she said, and bent over Thjodolf, who was dabbling his bun in her coffee cup.

"Well, fancy!" said Helene, and sat still. "Was this quite lately? Congratulations!" she added hastily.

"Thank you. It was two months ago," was the quick reply. "And you can't think what a nice husband I've got, Mrs. Johansen! Fancy, he's a foreigner—an Austrian—well, a Hungarian really, I believe. His name's Burg, so I'm Mrs. Burg now."

"That is," she whispered mysteriously, "that isn't his whole name—I can't say any more just now. But when peace comes— Oh, he's been through a lot, Rudolf has—terribly exciting, you know, but *dreadful*—and *so* interesting! He was in the war, you know, and got wounded and everything, but it was all so ghastly that he couldn't stand it any longer—and so now he daren't go back to Germany—Austria, rather

—not while the war's on, anyway. And so he's over in this country now, and has something to do with buying—fish, I think it is—and he writes in the papers too—" and so she went on talking and talking.

My goodness, thought Helene. Might have known she'd get mixed up in something shady.

"Well, the point *is*," said Fanny, squeezing the child to her, "what I really came to tell you—Rudolf, my husband, is mad about children, and what do you think, he wants us to have Thjodolf at home with us—" and she kissed the boy's hair passionately.

Helene sat speechless, incapable of thinking a single thought.

"I expect you'll miss him a bit at first," said Fanny comfortingly, "but you must come and see us, you know—mustn't she, Toddie? Helene tum and see us in town."

"We shan't have the flat ready for another week," she went on, "so I can't take him now. But in a week we thought we'd come down and fetch him—Rudolf and me, I mean."

"But you gave him away for good, to be brought up as our own child," said Helene softly. "So you must surely understand—you can't possibly take him back again just like that." And involuntarily she put out her hand to the child.

Thjodolf was sitting quietly and happily on his mother's lap, playing with her handbag.

"Ah, yes, that was *then*," said Fanny a little airily. "Why, at that time I was at my wit's end what to do or where to turn. But everything's different now."

Helene sat with her mouth open.

"But we took him to bring up as our own," she kept saying, tonelessly.

"But of course, my dear Mrs. Johansen, I know that—that was how it was then. But surely you realize that you can't refuse to let a mother have her own child—now, can you?—when circumstances are so changed that she can keep it."

Helene said nothing.

"Of course I know you'll feel it at first," said Fanny. "But, after all, you *are* only his foster mother, so it isn't as if he was your own. And being so fond of him yourself, you'll appreciate my feelings as his real mother."

Helene made no answer.

"Naturally I feel for you very much," the mother went on. "But as it's *my* child— And you know," she added brightly, "you'll have no trouble in finding another child—one that's lost its mother. I'd be glad to recommend you to the foster-child bureau."

Helene raised her eyes from Thjodolf's face to his mother's.

"I'm just wondering whether it's legal," she said, almost threateningly.

· · ·

Thjodolf's mother caught the midday boat back to town. Helene still couldn't take in all that had been said, either by herself or by the other woman. She was numb.

The little boy toddled about the room with his toys and Helene could hardly bring herself to touch him, as if she were afraid that every time she took hold of him she would come to love him even more.

That evening, after Thjodolf had fallen asleep, she knocked on the door of the sitting-room. The same two elderly ladies were staying with her as had come the year before. One of them worked in a government office. Helene told them what had happened and asked whether they thought she was bound to let the baby go.

Whether she was legally bound to do this Miss Sand could not say for certain, but she believed that by Norwegian law Helene could not refuse, as she had not formally adopted the boy. Morally, at any rate, she surely could not feel she had the right to withhold a child from its mother.

Helene murmured that there was another side to it—that the mother wasn't all she should be.

"But that's why!" the other lady—a schoolteacher —broke in. "That's it. There have been so many examples—and it's really a miracle to see how an irresponsible—a really *quite* irresponsible—girl can be saved when she's allowed to keep her baby. Nothing guards a woman from going astray so well as being allowed to be a mother to her child."

"And there are so many abandoned, helpless little ones that would give you an outlet for your maternal feelings, Mrs. Johansen. For every child you can adopt, twenty need your care."

Helene wrote to Julius that evening, telling him he must come home on Sunday, as she had something important to talk to him about.

But Julius said the same thing as the ladies in the sitting-room. If the mother wanted her kid back, they couldn't refuse. But mostly he talked about Fanny's marriage, which seemed to amuse him enormously. Whew, that just about suited her! Because of course there was something fishy about that Burg chap—he must be some sort of spy.

They were in the garden, for Julius felt that as he was here he might as well give the flagstaff another coat of paint. He laid it on the ground and went on painting it as he talked on and on about Fanny and Burg. Helene stood by him with Thjodolf on her arm; she was taciturn and hard-faced. The ladies leaned out of the window and gave their opinion, and again they said how easily Helene could find another baby in need of her care. Helene crushed the boy to her until he began to cry, and her face went even harder.

But Julius thought it was a good idea. This time they'd take care to have a child of really decent parents, then there wouldn't be all this fuss. They must get hold of one belonging to a real spinster lady, for one could be sure that people of that sort would never ask for it back.

Helene washed all Thjodolf's clothes, looked them over carefully, and packed them, all mended and neat, in two big cardboard boxes. Day after day went by; every morning Helene woke with the same feeling of tension and went about absorbed in her own thoughts, so that she hardly saw or heard the little boy, and did not answer his prattling.

When the week was up, Helene began to think that perhaps something had happened to prevent it; perhaps the husband had changed his mind. But again, perhaps not. She dared not dart at the child, talk to him, and play with him as in the days when she believed he was her own. But in the evenings when he had fallen asleep, Helene sat at the kitchen table staring out at the summer night with unseeing eyes, and almost holding her breath with suspense. Suppose it never—

Nearly three weeks passed, and then one day they came—Fanny and her husband. He was a fat little man with brown curly hair, brown whiskers, brown eyes, and a great many white teeth with bluish fillings in them. He looked kind; he smiled all the time and snapped his fingers at Thjodolf: *"Bubi! Bubi! Hübscher Bub!"* Fanny was radiant; so merry and lively that she couldn't keep still a minute.

Helene packed the last of Thjodolf's things and fetched his blue coat with the lion buttons and his sailor cap. Fanny put them on the boy.

"Say good-by nicely to Mummy Helene, now, Toddie. Go and give Mummy Helene a kiss, Bubi!"

But the boy didn't understand; he had no idea that he was to leave his home.

"Good-by, good-by," said Fanny Burg. "Thank you again so very much—and mind you come and see us soon. Good-by, good-by!"

The German bowed gallantly and smilingly. Then he took the little blue-clad figure on his arm. Fanny carried the boxes. And they went.

The window was open. Helene heard the boy beginning to cry; they were at the foot of the slope now. "Mummy!" cried Thjodolf. Helene stood in a corner of the room, pressed against the wall, and didn't look out.

7

TWICE Helene went to Christiania, meaning to go and see how Thjodolf was getting on. But she couldn't bring herself to do it. She walked along Sverdrups

Street, past the house where the Burgs were living, hoping she might see Thjodolf out on the pavement with the other children. But he wasn't there.

It was just as well, of course, that Fanny didn't let the tiny fellow out by himself; he might easily get run over or something. But when it came to the point, Helene couldn't bring herself to go up and see Fanny; she would have felt like a beggar.

So Helene did the things she had to do, and went home. She started for the cemetery, but turned back. She wondered whether to call on the Lunds, but decided she didn't feel up to it. She would have liked to ask Lawyer Lund a few questions—but then there was this business about the money. Julius had squandered all that they'd been given for Thjodolf, as well as the hundred crowns from the lawyer.

At last, on her third visit to the town, she did go and call on Mrs. Burg. She had dreamed about Thjodolf several times lately, and although she couldn't quite remember the dreams she had the impression that something was wrong, so that she woke with a feeling of dread.

It was a scorching day at the end of August, and the air in the streets was thick with dust. Warm, nasty smells filled the staircase where the Burgs lived. Helene had to wait for a long time after ringing the bell under the little brass plate that bore a foreign name. At last, after she had rung two or three times and was on the point of going away, the door opened a crack: it was on the chain.

"Why, it's you!" twittered Fanny's voice delightedly. She banged the door, undid the chain, and opened the door again wide. "How nice of you to call, Mrs. Johansen! Come along in. I thought you must have forgotten all about Toddie and me—please forgive the state we're in—I wasn't expecting visitors, as you can see."

She was in petticoat, stays, and a rather grubby chemise; and the same bedroom smell that came from her seemed to fill the room into which she showed Helene. There was a divan bed along one wall, unmade; the covers had just been smoothed over it a little.

Apart from the divan, the room was rather bare, though the few pieces of furniture in it seemed good. There was a very elegant writing-desk by one window—one of the American kind that Helene had seen displayed in the shops, with a roll-top to pull down and lock. On one windowsill stood a dead hothouse rose with crumpled tissue paper and ribbons round the pot; in the other window stood an open cardboard box overflowing with sewing-things.

Through an open door could be seen a bedroom that had not yet been tidied. Fanny ran in and came back at once with Thjodolf on her arm and a pink dressing-jacket in the other hand. The boy had evidently been roused from sleep that very moment; he whimpered and rubbed his eyes. His hair was soaked with sweat.

His mother sat him on the floor, put on the dressing-jacket, and tucked her hair into a little lace cap.

"Who's this, Thjodolf? Don't you remember Helene? Why, I really don't believe he knows you! Poor mite, he's so sleepy. Bubi—

"Everything's in such a state. I've been so dreadfully tired these last few days. We had someone staying here—a friend of my husband's—but now they've gone to Bergen, he and my husband; they left the day before yesterday, so I've been taking it easy since then. . . .

"Yes, poor mite, he looks a bit peaky today—yes, you're right, he doesn't look well. Oh, it's nothing serious, you know—just his tummy. It's this hot weather—and then he caught such a cold. We were out at Bygdønes my husband and his friend and me and the boy, and he got very hot that day, and it's a bit chilly in the evenings now."

She darted out into the passage and came in again with a raincoat over her jacket and petticoat, to look for money behind a few oddments on a shelf. Helene said something about not wanting to make trouble.

"Oh, we were going to have something ourselves, anyway. We haven't had dinner yet."

Helene stayed with the child.

"Thjodolf," she coaxed. "Thjodolf, my precious, don't you know me, then? Have you forgotten your mum?" she whispered, crouching down before the boy, who drew away from her.

It seemed so. The boy stood mute, with a finger in his mouth, looking at her. And, dear God, how he'd gone back! His face was yellowish-white and his dark curly hair clammy with sweat.

"Oh, my precious, precious boy!"

Fanny returned and put three small bottles of beer, a jug of milk, and a bag of Vienna bread on the table.

"I haven't a scrap of coffee in the house," she explained. "And it would have made it so late if I'd dressed and gone all the way to the grocer's. You'll have to take things as you find them."

Thjodolf toddled along the walls in such a funny way. Now and then he came up to his mother and drank from the cup of milk. Helene thought how he had been in the old days: she hadn't been able to sit down for a bite herself without his rushing to her crying: "Toddie sit Mummy's lap—Toddie taste Mummy's dinner!"

"Goodness, do you give him unboiled milk—when his tummy's upset, too!" exclaimed Helene, horrified.

But Fanny explained that that was just the reason. She had read somewhere that fresh milk was much more digestible than boiled milk, and much more nourishing, she said rather importantly. Though, indeed, there was little enough left of that rather superior air that Helene had noticed the last few times she had seen her. She was more as she had been during her worst period. Poor soul, there must be something wrong somewhere. At any rate she was genuinely delighted to see Helene.

"I think you should take him to the doctor," said Helene, whose eyes never left Thjodolf.

Fanny said that she had thought of it, but that it was so difficult for her to get away. And then the money. The clinic? Yes, but that was so early in the morning. And the money; she found it so hard to make ends meet. Rudolf said that he didn't know any town in Europe more expensive than Christiania. And his money came in so irregularly; sometimes they had more than enough, and at others they were really hard up. Fanny went on talking feverishly about her husband and his affairs, and boasting, and she hinted again at some secret about his name: he was a more important person than anyone dreamed. He was so kind; he had such fine manners. But Helene could see that she wasn't saying all this because she felt superior or happy, poor soul; quite the contrary.

At last Fanny came out with what was on her mind. She needed some things for the boy—Bubi, she called him—and she didn't feel she could ask

Ruddi—oh, not that he didn't like the boy: he adored him, and Helene mustn't think he didn't—but all the same, *you* know. In short, the bankbook in Thjodolf's name that Helene had once shown her—could Helene lend her the money in that account?

Helene looked at the pallid child—her baby, whatever the world might say, were the other woman fifty times his mother. He was wearing his pretty blue Sunday smock, and it was so filthy in front as to be really matted. And one knicker-leg hung down to the top of his boot. He had an old silk handkerchief tied round his neck, his nose was running, and his eyes were quite swollen from his cold.

Helene said yes, she would send the money the very next day, if Fanny would take Thjodolf to the doctor immediately. When she was leaving she took Thjodolf in her arms, wiped his nose thoroughly—wiped his whole pretty little face—and then kissed him well and warmly, three or four times.

Some weeks later she went into Christiania again to see Thjodolf. This time she took Julius along; she somehow felt that this would lend authority to the visit.

The child still had a cold, but he looked better. Fanny said she had taken him to the doctor, who assured her that there was nothing seriously the matter with the boy. The house was tidier, and Fanny was dressed. She was quite radiant with delight at this visit and asked them to stay and have dinner with her. She gave them sausages and beer followed by coffee. In a way it was all quite enjoyable—if only Thjodolf hadn't been so shy; he must have forgotten his foster parents altogether.

Burg wasn't at home this time either; he traveled about a great deal and was in Stockholm now, Fanny thought.

But when Helene rang the bell in Sverdrups Street one day at the end of September, no one answered. Burg's name-plate was still there, but when Helene inquired at the flat opposite, the woman there told her that the Burgs had left and that there were some other foreigners in the place now—three or four men whom no one in the house knew anything about. What had become of the Burgs she didn't know; she'd heard they were somewhere out Asker way, but they didn't seem too keen on people knowing their address. Yes, they'd paid the rent very punctual—it was handy for them, that flat, you know, whatever it was they wanted it for; there was goings-on enough there, the Lord knew. But they owed money in the shops round about. As to their being married—well, nobody in the house believed *that* tale, the woman said.

. . .

One afternoon in November, Mrs. Hansen at the shop persuaded Helene to go with her to a revivalist family who had a preacher visiting them from Christiania. They had coffee, and afterwards the preacher spoke—very well and beautifully, Helene thought. In general she didn't care for the to-do the revivalists made, but this man Løvstø talked so serenely and sensibly that Helene had something to think about as she went home.

It may have been half past ten when Helene took hurried leave of Mrs. Hansen at the foot of her own hill. It was nasty wet weather and pitch dark, so there was no temptation to linger in the road. Helene hastened up the slope and was just going to run up the porch steps when she sensed that something dark was pressed against the wall. She started.

"It's only me, Mrs. Johansen," said a thick, tearful voice, and Helene recognized Fanny Erdahl.

"Dear God—!"

The other stood up. Helene knew without seeing it that she had the child in her arms.

"Dear God," said Helene again; she ran up and unlocked the door. The other woman slunk in like a wet dog and stood just inside the door while Helene lit the lamp. She was holding Thjodolf in her arms, wrapped up in her raincoat.

"Never in all my days . . ." said Helene, and found no more words. But she went over and took the bundle; it was sopping wet on the outside.

"He's asleep," said his mother. "He's slept a long time." Her voice broke. "We've been waiting since six o'clock. I went over to the Hansens', but there was nobody there either."

Helene took the raincoat and the other outer clothes off Thjodolf without waking him. She laid him on the bed and untied his wet boots. Good God, how thin his legs were.

"Take off your things," she said to Fanny softly, "and I'll get some—"

She lit the stove, put on some coffee and milk, and hung out two blankets to warm. Then she went into the sitting-room, lit the stove there, and made up the bed. Not until all that had been seen to and she began getting food did she say to Fanny: "You'll stay the night, of course."

"Thank you," said Fanny meekly. She was in the rocking-chair, as so often before. Helene couldn't help thinking of a stray cat that finds its way home now and then when it's had too rough a time of it.

"I was thinking—I wanted to ask you whether you'd take Thjodolf again—just for a time. I can't manage to keep him now—" and she burst out sobbing.

Helene poured out the coffee and quietly pushed the food over to Fanny.

"Try to eat a little now," she said gently, and just

stroked the other's arm.

Little by little Fanny grew calm enough to tell her story, weeping all the time. Burg had gone to Stockholm in September, and she hadn't seen him since. At first he'd sent her money once or twice, and a few letters, but she couldn't read German. He could speak a little Norwegian and she a little German, but she hadn't understood much of his letters. Then some other Germans came—or Finns—who were to move into her flat, and they made her move out to Asker, where she was to live with a German woman, the wife of one of them. But it hadn't worked; they lived miserably there, and the German lady had been a horrible old hag. Then at last, a few days ago, she had heard that Rudolf had gone back to Germany and the German lady had been insolent to her and thrown her out.

And now at last she admitted that she'd never been properly married to Rudolf. He had told her he couldn't marry until after the war, because of his papers. But he had promised so faithfully, and he'd been so kind and affectionate, and so madly in love at the beginning—well, all the time, in fact.

Fanny cried a great deal and wallowed in memories of Burg. Now and then she talked about Thjodolf's father too, and her experiences with him. Helene had never known anyone like this: Fanny seemed unable to grasp that men were irresponsible and careless. She seemed to expect that any man who spoke to her would feel obliged to take care of her, as she couldn't take care of herself. What a creature! But it was very hard on her, poor soul.

At last Helene got her settled in the sitting-room. Thjodolf was in the double bed in the kitchen, and he woke up when Helene came in and lay down beside him. She gave him milk and bread, and he ate with a good appetite; and he was warm now, for she had tucked him up in hot blankets. But he wouldn't lie still with her; he cried and called for Mummy, so at last Helene had to take him in to Fanny.

Fanny stayed for three days. She would probably have liked to remain longer, but Helene behaved as if expecting her to leave. Fanny had absolutely no plans for her future; did Helene think she could get a situation in Drøbak? But Helene was sure she couldn't; instead, she advised her to go and make it up with her aunt, and then perhaps she could get some sewing to do, for Fanny had taken a course in dressmaking in the old days.

Two days after Fanny left, Helene was down in the garden hanging out Thjodolf's underclothes, which she had mended and washed. They had come back in a shocking state—as many as did come back.

The boy was toddling about out there, for it was fine weather for the time of year; the air was mild and moist, and a glint of sun came now and then to gild the grassplots in the garden. The fir trees on the ridge behind the house shone olive-green against the sky, which was a dark gray-blue, with drifting rain clouds.

Suddenly Thjodolf came and pulled at Helene's skirt. He had something in his hand and he held it up to her, his little face alight with smiles.

"Mummy, Mummy, look—Lakel!" he said.

It was his old wooden horse, which he had found somewhere in the bushes. All the paint had come off it; it was covered with dirt, and withered leaves were sticking to it.

The boy stretched his arms up to Helene and said: "Hop-la, Mummy—hop-la!"

Helene sank to her knees on the ground and gathered him in. She hugged him and hugged him to her breast, and the tears came, so that something seemed to have broken in pieces deep inside her, and a wave welled over. She herself didn't realize that never in her life had she wept like this, and that all the tears she had never shed were flowing now.

8

SHE was not quite aware, either, that during the winter that followed she was different, and her whole life was different from anything that had gone before. Day followed day, full of deep joy and of a hidden, heart-rending anxiety.

Tiny Thjodolf began to remember one or two other things from their former life together. One day he stood for a long time looking at the sewing-machine; then he touched the shiny wheel, and immediately afterwards slapped his own fingers with the other hand: "Ah, mustn't!" as Helene had sometimes done when he wouldn't let her sew in peace. He went over to the stove and put out his hand without touching it. "Ah, ah, ah, mustn't!" And he said "Hop-la, Mummy," and "Sit Mummy's lap" when there was food to be had.

And he was learning all the time: almost every day there was something, and he was so good and sweet and funny that Helene was dizzy with joy over her child.

He *was* her child. Never again would she let him go. She thought how Fanny Erdahl might come along one day and demand to have him back, and her face went hard and cruel. She thought of what she would say: it wouldn't be pleasant. She would remind her of the two men she had lived with, and of that business of the accounts out at Grønland; she would ask whether Fanny thought that a person who couldn't look after herself was fit to look after a child. Oh, no, never again should that woman get her hands on him. She had done the boy enough harm as it was, for Thjodolf had suffered a setback while he was with her.

That was the word the doctor used: a setback, he said. The boy's stomach was in a wretched state, and he had bronchitis. But the doctor said too that good nursing would set him up again all right.

And Helene did nurse him, so she had time for little more than that and her regular housework. Only four crowns had been entered in the new bank-book by February. She made thick carrot-and-kale soup, and water gruel and rye gruel; milk he was not allowed to have for the present, and he was so fond of it and begged so hard for it that often Helene was on the edge of tears at having to deny it him. She rubbed his back and chest with warm oil, and when his cough was bad she had to lie in bed with him in the daytime, for unless she did he wouldn't stay under the covers. She lay there half undressed, and played with him and sang to him, and stole away to do the housework while he slept. There was no question now of her slipping him a tidbit to keep him quiet; chocolate and sweet things were absolutely forbidden.

So when he was whiny and fractious Helene had to play with him and sing to him for hours on end.

He tried her very hard, but grew ever more deeply attached to her at the same time.

Then spring came on. Helene rejoiced, for as soon as Thjodolf could be out every day he would be bound to get stronger. She hummed as she made him a new jacket; the blue one that he had gone back to his own mother in was in such a dreadful state that she decided to make him a new one out of her old winter coat. The stuff was as good as new, though the style was very old-fashioned now. It would be nice to make a new coat for herself in the autumn. She planned how she would make it. Navy blue . . . Perhaps she would cut up the old fur stole and use it to trim the coat.

Thjodolf had been coughing again lately. And one night, after a long coughing-fit she heard him whooping.

The first, mild days of May had come, and the grassplot down in the garden was turning green. The rhubarb plants thrust their thick, lacquer-red shoots up out of the soil; the peonies raised their curly brown leaves between the gray, withered sticks of last year's stalks; and in the bed under the sitting-room window the shoots of the daffodils stood close, like little green knife-points. Helene saw it all from the window, and her tears ran down for Thjodolf, who lay so pale and wretched in bed when he ought to have been out in the fine weather.

He was really ill, poor little man; he coughed and whooped until he could hardly get his breath, and he couldn't keep his food down. On the doctor's advice she had moved into the big sitting-room with him. She stayed by him night and day, holding his forehead, supporting him during his paroxysms of coughing, and feeding him with custard or broth in small helpings in the hope that he might keep it down.

On the fifteenth of May, in the evening, he developed a high fever. Helene telephoned from Mrs. Hansen's for the doctor, and when he came he told her that pneumonia had set in.

"Do you think he'll come through it?" asked Helene, her terrified eyes on the young doctor's face.

"There's always hope," he said softly, but Helene heard his tone and saw his face, and was inwardly frantic.

For a night and a day and a night and another day Helene fought for her precious boy's life. On the third night he was still alive, and she lay fully dressed beside him on the bed. She renewed the hot compresses on the fevered little body and the cold ones on his burning forehead. Perhaps she ought not to have lain there; it made it too warm for him, but it seemed to soothe the boy to feel her near him. He could no longer speak, but he gripped her hands and arms and clothes and clung there, when he was at all conscious.

During his last struggle he lay in Helene's arms. But in the morning, when there was daylight outside and the starlings were piping in the garden, Thjodolf died.

That evening, when Helene left the beautiful, be-decked little body in the sitting-room, meaning to lie down in the kitchen for a little, she saw that there were blue-and-green bruises on her arms where Thjo-dolf's little fingers had clutched her in the death struggle.

Julius came down to the funeral with Fanny Erdahl. The mother looked unspeakably tear-stained and wretched under her crape veil. She gave the impres-sion of being utterly distraught, although she was fairly well turned out in her new black clothes. She had found a good situation at a dressmaker's out at Grünerløkken, it seemed. And once more Helene thought of a stray cat. She realized that Fanny had had something weighing on her mind before Thjo-dolf's death. Helene looked after her as well as she could, and had prepared the attic room for her, not wanting to put her in the sitting-room where Thjo-dolf had died. But she found little to say to her.

On the day of the funeral it rained. The church-yard was dreary in the extreme: the little group of mourners stood under umbrellas round the open grave. When the earth trickled from the pastor's shovel through the wreaths onto the coffin, Helene had to support the mother's arm; Fanny looked as if she would fall headlong, and she groaned like an animal in pain.

Helene herself could not weep. Her soul seemed to have been wrung out of her body during the last days. The mourners came back to the house and Helene got the dinner: roast veal and layer cake which she had baked the day before. These were the dishes she had meant to prepare for Thjodolf's confirmation party; Helene herself hardly knew why she had chosen to serve them now—perhaps it was to try and bring her pain back to life and to feel that her heart was not altogether dead, that she could still weep to remember all she had dreamed of for her boy. She remembered as she cooked, peeled potatoes, and made sauce, but the tears did not come.

In the evening the rain stopped. There was a heavenly fragrance of birch buds and the sweaty smell of the bird-cherry shoots when Helene stood on the steps of the porch and said good-by to her guests. Fanny offered to help her with the washing-up, but Helene said no thank you; instead, Fanny and Julius went a little way with their visitors. Among these were relations of Julius's, who lived out beyond Husvik.

Helene had washed up and tidied the house, and now sat by the window staring listlessly out into the spring night. The fjord gleamed softly under the cloudy sky; the treetops were still transparent, but were beginning to grow denser; everywhere buds were on the point of bursting. A scent of earth and growth wafted in from the garden, where a bird here and there was still awake and singing.

She would divide her auriculas—it ought to have been done this spring, anyway—and plant a thick wreath of them on the grave. Her throat tightened and her eyes smarted, but the feeling passed at once. No tears came when she tried to think of Thjodolf's grave.

Listlessly she rose and stole through the porch into the open. For a time she stood inhaling the cool, damp night air—then wandered about at random. She went over to the corner of the house and looked downhill toward the road and the fjord.

Two people were coming up the slope, walking close together. After a few steps they stopped, put their arms about each other, and stood in close embrace.

Helene glided back into the shadow of the house. Then she ran silently indoors, her knees trembling under her, and sank down on her usual chair by the window. Her chemise stuck to her body: she was in a cold sweat.

A little later Fanny and Julius came in.

"You ought to a' come with us," said her husband. "It's a wonderful fine evening."

Helene could not utter a word; she was searching within her mind for phrases bitter enough, sneering and coarse enough. She groped among memories of her distant girlhood in the town for the filthy, vulgar expressions she had learned then—learned but passed by, her nose in the air, pretending not to hear them. They were in her throat, but she bit them back nevertheless.

Julius was over by the stove, shaking the kettle.

"There ain't a drop left, I s'pose?"

Instinctively Helene started to bestir herself, to do her duty as housewife. But her whole body was twitching—she felt she dared not venture across the floor, or she would do something terrible.

"I've washed up once this evening," she said thickly.

"Why, my dear, I can rinse these cups out myself—" and then Fanny met Helene's eyes. She slipped back into the rocking-chair, and her face, still blotchy with weeping, turned pale: Helene looked so queer.

"I think I must go straight to bed," Fanny said faintly, a moment later. "I'm so worn out—I'm really at the end of my tether." Her voice was stifled by crying. She felt Helene's eyes stabbing her back as she slunk out, broken and sobbing.

"Ay, ay, poor soul," said Julius, sitting down at the table with a cup of tepid, muddy coffee. "It's been hard for her, all this."

Helene never moved. Her voice was level with suppressed passion as she said without looking up: "It was just an act of charity, I suppose, when you were comforting her just now."

Julius gaped.

"I saw you coming up the slope," said Helene, as before.

"Oh. That." Julius fidgeted in his seat, and his face turned dark red. "*That—*" he said quickly. "You know very well that was just a bit of nonsense. She was in such a state—I had to pat her a little—nothing for *you* to worry about."

The storm in Helene suddenly sank to calm again. Of course. She couldn't think why she had taken it like that. It was just a bit of nonsense, and she ought to be used to that by now—used to Julius fooling with girls. Why should it trouble her any more? But now that her mind was tired and cold, her voice rang out sharply and excitedly: "I don't know how you can, Julius—what you can see in a creature like that—a flibbertigibbet who's been with one man after another—ugh!"

"Ah, now look here," said Julius in an injured

tone. "I wasn't doing it for fun, you know—the poor girl was nearly out of her mind."

"I'm not surprised. She's got something to cry for, and that's a fact. She's in the family way again."

Julius reddened darkly again.

"How can you tell—?"

Helene sent him a look sparkling with scorn. Misconstruing it, he stood up.

"Ay, ay, Helene—it's a bad business, true enough. It was treating you shabby, I know. But you got to remember this. It ain't been easy for a chap living away from home the way I do—like a gay bachelor. And she was forever hanging about and making up to me like, as coaxing as a kitten. And it's years now since you was so gentle to me—enough to notice, anyhow. Fair's fair, and you got to remember that—"

Helene stood bolt upright; she seemed turned to stone, and her face was so white that it gleamed.

"—Well, I know I done wrong. But you ain't always been such an angel to me, you know. And if you *are* too good for me, you've made me feel it often enough. I always knew the others was nothing beside you, but—"

Helene screamed—a single, long, piercing, animal scream.

"Christ!" said Julius, and moved toward her.

She turned to face him; she was frantic.

"Get away with you, you—you— Go, d'you hear

me? Go up to her—go up to your whore, you bit of filth! Jesus Christ, I can't stand the sight of you—I—"

She darted past him, flung open the door of the sitting-room, slammed it behind her, and turned the key. For a time she stood with her hand on it, her whole body shaking. Then she reeled the two or three steps to the bed and threw off the blanket and eider-down; and as she knelt, twisting and rubbing her head and shoulders into the bedclothes, the weeping came, bitter and burning. She hugged the pillow on which Thjodolf had died, crushed it to her, and in her infinite anguish cried upon Jesus and her child.

MISS SMITH–TELLEFSEN

"Yes, you'll just have to make
the best of what there is. Oh
dear, I'm afraid the coffee's
thick. I ought to have gone out
and made it myself, I suppose,
but I did so want to stay and
chat with you, Mrs. Storaker.
It's wonderful to have a visitor
for once. *Oh,* that Serianna! These mountain girls,
you know, you just can't get them to learn a thing.
And what about you? Has Randi Høgste come to you
yet? How do you think you're going to like her? I expect it'll be the same old bother—"

"Well, no," the pastor's wife said gently and cheer-
fully. "Do you know, Miss Smith, I really don't think
she's going to be so bad. Of course, after coping with
someone like Kari, I'm easily pleased. But there's one
thing—she is good with the children. You can imagine how much that means in a household like ours.
And my husband likes her so much. They're such excellent people, those Høgste folk, you know; my husband thinks very highly of them."

"Yes, indeed. How beautifully Lars Høgste spoke,
that evening we went there for the prayer meeting! I
said to Mr. Biørn afterwards, you ought to have come,
I said. *Such* a pity he cares so little for those things;

but, you know, he seems to have no spiritual aspirations at all. Isn't it strange? He certainly doesn't have an easy life of it up here in the wilds, with those long journeys to Blåfjell mine in all weathers. And the miners—such horrid, trying, grasping men to deal with. Not a single educated person for him to meet, except when you and the pastor . . . It's so lovely to see you, Mrs. Storaker—such a pity the pastor hadn't time to look in. We so much enjoyed the evening you came here after the Høgste meeting; why, Mr. Biørn and I were quite stimulated for a long time afterwards. Do have another cake, Mrs. Storaker; I'm afraid they're not quite as they should be—a little too much soda—but I don't think the *Berlinerkranser* [1] are too bad, though I say it myself. Really? How kind. I don't believe you'd ever guess I'd used preserved eggs—wonderful how they kept; I had some of them right up to June. Mr. Biørn had a boiled one every Sunday and often at other times too—when he came back from Blåfjell and so on—and they were delicious; but d'you know the shells went terribly brittle; I had to boil them myself, of course, and they would always crack in the hot water. Is there anything one can do about that? Put them in when the water's cold? Yes, well, I did think of trying that. . . .

"But wouldn't you think that anyone in Mr. Biørn's position would feel a need for spiritual things? It

---

[1] A small, dry cake which keeps a long time.

seems to me as if God might so easily get hold of him
—but Mr. Biørn's not *like* that. He felt the loss of his
wife so terribly—why, it's over two years now since
she passed on, and I don't believe a day goes by but
what he thinks of her; not that he says anything, you
know, but I often catch him looking at her picture—
sometimes he does it when we're sitting here together
in the evenings, and I feel really sorry for him. Yes, as
you see, I've arranged some dwarf birch round the
picture; I always put something. Last winter I had
some spruce sent up, but even that didn't rouse him."

"No, it's strange how some people are. As you say,
Miss Smith, they seem not to feel any need for spiritual things—that's very true. Dear me, yes, you may
be sure my husband's noticed it since we came here.
Down in Kjørrefjord, where we were before, there
was such an active religious life. But the people up
here seem to me utterly apathetic and indifferent to
spiritual matters, both peasants and miners—so
wrapped up in worldly things that really I've never
seen anything like it. My poor husband often feels
most depressed about it—it's pitiful to see. I know
he's tried several times to talk to Mr. Biørn—"

"And yet, it's not that Mr. Biørn isn't a spiritual
kind of man; I believe he is, and very much so. But
he's somehow so odd and reserved and never will talk
to anyone about himself. I've tried to make him speak
of his wife, for instance, but he won't. I thought it

would be good for him, for I'm certain not a day goes by without him thinking of her. I don't know whether he ever speaks of her to the children; I asked Laila that the other day: 'Does Daddy ever talk to you about Mummy?' I asked her, but she wouldn't answer. Laila's strange that way—"

"Takes after her father, perhaps?"

"I don't know whether it isn't more the mother. Mr. Biørn is oddly reserved, of course, but Laila's somehow so— Mr. Biørn is really very affectionate and kind, and do you know I really believe he has a very soft heart. When I think how he was with his wife! Bikku was well on the way when I came here, and after he was born she was terribly ill; she was in bed for most of the time that was left to her, poor thing, so one couldn't expect her to be so wonderfully good-tempered. I know *I* could never do anything to please her, though I tried my very best—and I thought she was really nasty to her husband, poor man, and he just couldn't do enough for her—my goodness, what a fuss he made of her! But she took it all for granted. Often I thought she was really odd —she was almost cruel to him—Mr. Biørn who did everything for her."

"She was from the north, wasn't she?"

"Yes, from Finnmark. But she'd worked in an office in Christiania for some years. That's what she didn't like: having to live up here. What I say is that if one marries one must just take the consequences and be content to live wherever one's husband has his work; and even if one does feel that there are rather too many children coming along, I don't think that's any reason to make oneself unpleasant to one's husband."

Her back was turned, for she was fetching a bottle of bilberry wine and some glasses from the sideboard, so she missed Mrs. Storaker's smile—the pitying smile with which married women always receive the remarks of spinsters on the subject of married life and all that pertains to it.

"No, I just don't know. So often I feel it's too dull and dreary here to be borne. When it's weather like this—ugh, just listen to it! You'd think the house was going to blow away—poor Mr. Biørn, what weather to be out driving in! I think it was so brave of you, Mrs. Storaker, to come up here with the pastor. I was delighted to see you; I was really feeling quite depressed; did you ever hear such rain? I must say I'm longing to get down among people again. Sometimes I feel tempted to find another situation, and leave here, but I don't really feel I can. I'm used to the place, and it wouldn't be easy for poor Mr. Biørn to get anyone else to come up here—and you never know how she'd get on with him or the children or the house. No, I couldn't bring myself to do it—to go to him and give notice—why, I feel it would be a mean thing to do. It's as if I had a duty to perform here."

"Ah, here's Laila," said Mrs. Storaker.

A little eight-year-old girl came clumping in, in *beksøm* [2] boots. She had a stiff yellow braid and a square, heavy face.

"Say how do you do nicely to Mrs. Storaker, Laila dear."

Laila wriggled a little and shook hands. Then she helped herself to some *Berlinerkranser* from the dish and dumped herself down in an armchair.

"Can I have some coffee, Miss Smith?"

"Go up and change your shoes first, dear. They must be soaked. Pooh, how you do smell of the cow-shed, Laila!"

"Can't be bothered. My boots are only wet on the outside, anyhow."

"Now dear, up you go. And put on a pinafore. Run along up at once, and ask Serianna to come and light the fire here. Nice to have a bit of fire, don't you think so, Mrs. Storaker? It'll make it a little cosier for Mr. Biørn too, when he gets in."

"Yes, it's beastly cold in here," said Laila as she flounced sulkily out of the room.

"She's such a difficult child," said Miss Smith-Tellefsen. "I always try to appeal to the best in her, you know—"

Laila came back in blue list slippers and a blue pinafore. Miss Smith-Tellefsen poured some bilberry wine into a third glass.

2 Heavy, stitched boots, without nails or pegs.

"Here you are, Laila—are you cold, dear? You shall have a little drop of wine, just for a treat. Let's feel your stockings—are they dry?"

"Well, what do you say, Laila?" It was the pastor's wife speaking. "Aren't you lucky! Tullik and Ruth never have wine, except on Christmas Eve."

"It's not her wine, it's daddy's," muttered Laila. Mrs. Storaker ignored this.

"Miss Smith-Tellefsen is always so good to you children."

"Well, she's paid to be."

Little Miss Smith-Tellefsen started up, her dough-gray face crimson.

"Oh, you insolent child!" She snatched the wine-glass from Laila's hand and gave her a sound smack on the cheek. "Go up to the nursery at once. You ought to be ashamed. I shall tell your daddy how you behave."

"And I'll tell him you hit me."

Laila disappeared, and Miss Smith-Tellefsen sank down on the sofa, still red in the face. There was a painful silence.

"I never heard such a rude child," said Mrs. Storaker.

"Yes, well, now you can see what she's like. What I have to put up with—" and Miss Smith-Tellefsen burst into tears. "That's how she goes on all the time. I try to be as good to her as I can, but, oh dear, Mrs. Storaker, life's no bed of roses when you have to go

1 5 3

out and earn your living among strangers. Mrs. Biørn
was just the same; so long as you were getting paid for
it she could never find enough for you to do—and not
a word of thanks, however hard you worked. Bikku at
night, mending the children's clothes, teaching Laila
to read, darning curtains and linen, and keeping an
eye on everything—and on top of it all the endless
cooking. No, I don't think twenty crowns a month
was much for all that."

"Yes, I must say I've admired you many a time,"
Mrs. Storaker said warmly. "But, my dear Miss Smith,
you must be better off now, in several ways. You can
run the house almost as if it were your own, and
Mr. Biørn does so appreciate all you do. You mustn't
let that child distress you."

"No, and I don't complain, you know. Although, I
must say, it's lonely and dreary enough here very often. For anyone with the recommendations I have, it
oughtn't to be difficult to find something better. I'm
lively by nature, there's no denying, and often I long
for some place with more life in it—young people in
the house, and so on. I remember when I was with the
Pettersens. Many a time I've almost regretted leaving
them—and they did so want me to stay on—they positively begged me to. All the same I feel it's my duty to
be here; I'm almost in the place of a mother to these
children. But you can see how wounding it is when
Laila shows she doesn't care a scrap about me, in spite

of all I do. Oh, she's so naughty and rude, and she puts little Biørn up to it too. No, if it weren't for Mr. Biørn and little Bikku . . . It would be hard to leave Bikku. He's so sweet and good, Mrs. Storaker. You ought to see him in the mornings when he wakes and wants to come into my bed—how he stretches out his fat little arms. I don't see how one could love a child more, even if it were one's own. I'm sure I couldn't. And I say to him: 'Who are you, Bikku?' and he puts his arms round my neck and says: 'Åsta's silly-billy.' Yes, you must come up and see him before you go. If only he could shake off that cold of his. But he does seem to be a little delicate, and this is such a harsh climate. I've had him to myself ever since he was born, you know, and looked after him from the first night."

"Yes, you have a great responsibility here," said the pastor's wife.

"That's just how I feel. I really think I've got the house looking quite nice now. I can assure you it's very different from what it was when I came." She looked complacently round the big room with its unpainted paneling. "Mrs. Biørn didn't seem to have the knack of making places comfortable and nice. Oh, it *was* dismal! Nothing on the walls but these pictures of Sulitelma, and that high-school group. Have you looked at that, by the way? Oh, you must. *Isn't* Mr. Biørn handsome there—quite an Adonis. And not a flower, not a table mat, not an antimacassar. All those things are my doing, and I embroidered the covers in my own room too. The *étagère* and the ornaments on it, and those two vases on the table, and these blue cups—they're all mine, every one of them. I'd collected quite a lot of things one way and another. So I put them in here; as I said to Mr. Biørn, this is where I always sit. And besides, with Bikku sleeping in my room, anything I kept there would get knocked over. I planted some cuttings too, and made Mr. Biørn buy carpets and the two green plush chairs, at the auction when Pastor Hellesnaes died. I just can't do without a little comfort round me; I think it makes *such* a difference . . .

"No, it wouldn't seem right to leave now and hand everything over to a stranger. And housekeeping's no easy matter up here, you know. Why, the bottling and preserving alone . . . Do you know, I did twenty-seven screw-tops of meat balls last year, and ten fish puddings—trout, they were, and believe me, they were delicious. And then all the salting and smoking and curing, and the jams and vegetables to be seen to, if one's to have any variety. Twenty jars of rhubarb in water—it kept beautifully, and was just like fresh —and cranberries, sweet and sour, in water and syrup.

"Do you know, I found the most delicious veal at Sandstøen this week. I *was* pleased! Some of it I preserved, of course, but we had the sweetbreads in puff pastry on Sunday and the liver on Monday, and this Sunday we'll have the roast. Last night I was up till all hours making mock turtle, and Mr. Biørn will have it when he comes home this evening. How I wish you and the pastor could come—I've done it so beautifully with madeira sauce and diced root-vegetables and fried brain balls, for he's so fond of that, and some delicate little meat balls and fish balls—that's something I always take care to have in the house. Yes, I'm so looking forward to giving it to Mr. Biørn . . .

"By the way, I'm having some French beans up from Christiania; would you care for some at the same time? I can get them for one crown ten a thousand—I thought of getting five thousand; they're such good things to have . . .

"Goodness gracious, if the pastor isn't here already! How time does fly when one's having a good talk."

Driven by the gusts of wind, the clouds were rolling in over the slopes on the opposite side of the valley; in a moment the wet, gray blanket had blotted out the little farmhouses at the fringe of the woods and the summer cottages higher up. A broad, golden flood of evening sunshine bathed the crag where the engineer's house stood, as far as the narrow, blueblack chasm of the valley. The bare rock and heather and scrub, and the pools near the house, glittered in the sunshine. Farther across the plateau lay two little mountain fields with green meadowland about them; there was the yellow villa built in the Swiss style and, a little farther on, the dark cluster of buildings near the mine, with only the upland heath, vast and bare and grayish-yellow, surrounding them on all sides. The line of power pylons strode away across the hill until they vanished, tiny and forlorn, in the wilderness.

Miss Smith-Tellefsen stood on the steps and waved to the pastor and his wife until they disappeared down the slope. The wine had brought color to her cheeks; she had talked herself into smiles, and her eyes were happy.

"She's not really so terribly plain," said Mrs. Storaker to her husband. "And she's very capable. Poor thing, I really wish something might come of her and Mr. Biørn."

Bikku was asleep when she went up to the little attic room that she shared with him. She felt the boy's cheek with the back of her hand—how hot he was! He tossed a little when she touched him, but didn't wake.

Miss Smith-Tellefsen drew the curtains, lit the lamp on the bedside table, took off her blouse, and sat down in front of the looking-glass. She glanced at the child's bed, for there were certain details of Miss Smith-Tellefsen's toilet which not even Bikku was allowed to see. He was sleeping soundly, and she removed the three rolls from the top of her head, combed them out meticulously, and rolled them up again. Then she laid them carefully down on the dressing-table and arranged her own grayish-yellow wisps over the hair-pad. This took a long time. Next she took the rolls and tried them here and there about her head—a little farther forward, a little farther back —until she decided on their position and pinned them firmly in place. She smiled at herself in the glass, pleased with the result.

She pulled her chemise a little, this way and that, and smiled again. Her arms, shoulders, and breast were a little overblown and flabby, but her skin was youthfully white and soft. Miss Smith-Tellefsen was very proud of her figure. But the skin of her face lay wan and puffy over her flat features, and formed pouches under her small, gentle, light brown eyes. With that broad, flat nose and long upper lip taut over the strongly curved row of teeth, she looked rather like a friendly little monkey. But her neck was the worst. The whole of one side, from the ear downwards, had been eaten up by glands; nothing was left of the skin but dead white scars and swollen, purple weals.

For this reason, Åsta Smith-Tellefsen had a whole drawerful of neck finery. Now, having put on a bright, red silk blouse covered with black net, she chose a broad, black velvet ribbon to go round her throat, tied it in a fine large bow on the blemished side, and pinned a bunch of violets there. This almost completely covered the scars. She smiled contentedly again as she pinned the large gilt *sølje* [3] brooch at her bosom.

She went over and looked at the child once more. Poor little man; but it couldn't be anything serious, for he was sleeping so soundly. Sleeping the fever off, no doubt.

She walked through Biørn's bedroom to the nursery. Little Biørn was having his supper, but Laila's plate had not been touched; the little girl was kneeling on a chair coloring a picture in a painting-book with crayons.

"Finished, Lillebiørn? Bye-byes now? Oh, how tired we are!" She clapped her hands at him. "Now then, Laila, put away your things and have your supper, so you can get to bed."

"You promised I could have supper with Daddy when he came in."

"If you were good, I said. Do you think you've been good? First you tore your skirt this morning, so I shall have to sit up half the night mending it—and then you were very rude and behaved very badly—"

"I shan't go to bed until Daddy comes," said Laila.

"—but I suppose you think that because I'm paid for it you can tear everything to bits whenever you

[3] A silver pin worn on native costumes.

want to. You think I haven't enough to do as it is, and so I must sit up and sew and darn your things all night." Miss Smith-Tellefsen had reddened again and she pulled off Biørn's jersey with a hard hand. "Just you wait till *you* grow up, Laila, and have to earn your own living."

"Pooh—I shall marry when I grow up."

"Oh yes, somebody's bound to ask you—such a nice girl, so kind!"

Laila ran to the window and listened. "There's Daddy!" She dashed out and down the stairs.

Miss Smith-Tellefsen washed Biørn and got him into his sleeping-suit; but she didn't joke with him as usual. The boy was drowsy, too, and could hardly find his way through Our Father.

The engineer was standing with his back to the stove, warming himself, when she came down. Laila was on the sofa, busy with her doll.

"Good evening, Miss Smith-Tellefsen. Is supper ready? I'm famished. Foul weather, isn't it?"

"I thought perhaps you'd like to change first; I've had a fire lit in your room. Supper will be ready in a moment."

"I can't be bothered to change," said Biørn. "Let's just have something to eat, may we?"

"Run out and tell her, will you, Laila? But I do think it's rash of you, Mr. Biørn. It's so easy to catch a chill. Poor little Bikku's got such a cold, and I can't think how he caught it. Poor little man, he was coughing so this morning; it was really dreadful to hear him. I put him to bed straight after his dinner, so he'll be all right again by morning, I expect. Well, come along then!" Serianna brought in the mock turtle.

Biørn lounged over to the table, and Laila came and sat down beside him.

"Oh, Serianna, would you please bring Laila's supper down from the nursery? I just couldn't get her to bed, Mr. Biørn. She insisted on staying up and having supper with you."

"So you waited for Daddy, did you?" said Biørn, stroking her hair. Laila rubbed kittenishly against his hand. "I hope you've been good while I've been away?"

Laila didn't answer and neither did Miss Smith-Tellefsen.

"What, trouble again?"

There was a pause. Then Miss Smith-Tellefsen said: "For one thing Laila has torn her best skirt. No wonder, when she climbed the fence at Øifjell in it."

"You shouldn't let the children wear their Sunday clothes every day, you know. They must be able to romp about."

"That's just it: she took it without permission, or I wouldn't have said anything."

"Can't you lock things up, then?"

"And that's not all. But never mind that now. We're not going to bother you with things like that as soon as you come home. What sort of trip did you have, Mr. Biørn? How was it at Blåfjell today?"

"Oh, same as usual."

"Mrs. Storaker was up here. The pastor came to visit the workman who was so badly injured. That poor man—he's really bad."

"It's Evensen's own fault. Those men are so careless with dynamite—they handle it as if it were plug tobacco. And the company has all the trouble."

"I thought it was splendid of Mrs. Storaker to come up here in this weather. I was so sorry you happened to be away; they're such nice people, and it was really a joy to see them here."

She prattled on while Biørn ate his mock turtle and his pudding in silence. Miss Smith-Tellefsen set aside some of the pudding on two plates.

"That's for Biørn and Bikku tomorrow; I had to promise them some. Just fancy, Bikku heard me say I was going to make it, and he came toddling down in his nightshirt after the raisins—little rascal! The things that boy gets up to!"

Laila said goodnight. Biørn took his coffee cup over to the sofa table and sat down with a book and his pipe. Presently Miss Smith-Tellefsen came in again and seated herself in the armchair, drawing it nearer to him and to the lamp.

"So awkward, sewing dark material by lamplight."

"Leave it till the morning, then," he said from the depths of his book.

"That's easy to say!" She laughed gently. "With all the stockings and socks to do, *and* the washing. I've made good use of my time while you've been away, I can tell you. But this *weather!* I dried the socks and some of the children's clothes in the kitchen. But the big wash— What's the weather going to do, Mr. Biørn? You always seem to know. I've noticed you're nearly always right. I don't know how you do it."

"I'm afraid it'll be about the same," he said, without looking up.

"Oh dear, I suppose so. But I'm disturbing you, I know. I'll be quiet now. One gets so chatty when there's nobody to talk to—when one's alone all day. Mrs. Storaker says it's the same with her. Do you know, when I was with the Pettersens I could go all day without opening my mouth. They often asked me if there was anything the matter, and I'd never even noticed it—there was so much going on all round me, you know. Well, I won't disturb you any more."

"I think I'll go up now, anyway. I'm tired." He shut the book and stood up.

"Yes, that's right. I expect you are. Good night, then, Mr. Biørn. Sleep well."

"And you."

"Oh, by the way—how did you like the parsley roots with the mock turtle? I hadn't done it before, but I thought it would be nice to try. It seemed to me quite good."

"Yes, it was. Good night."

Biørn lay awake for some hours. That woman had lit such a huge fire in his room that he'd had to open the window—and then get up and shut it again, for the wind had risen until it threatened to tear the casement from its hinges. And the soapstone stove glowed on.

This damned house! It was so badly built that you could hear every sound in it. She was up again, seeing to the boy. He must have been talking in his sleep, or perhaps had waked up.

Biørn lay down again and stared into the darkness. She was really good to the children. Good and capable. A respectable person. Much too good for—

Besides, he didn't really like her. Affected old chatterbox; she maddened him with her ceaseless babbling. The way she cajoled him—rubbed herself against him, as it were. And when he thought of that neck of hers he shuddered. And yet at the same time she did have a certain effect on him. . . .

Now and then he wished that he had put an end to it. Then it would be done with, at any rate, and he'd have some peace.

Pad—pad—pad. She was shuffling about in there, barefoot or in stockings. She was right by his door.

Good God! He started up in bed, trembling. She was fumbling with the key—now she was turning it!

The light broke in harshly. Miss Smith-Tellefsen was standing in the doorway.

"Oh, Mr. Biørn, Mr. Biørn! Please come—I'm afraid there's something really wrong with Bikku. Please come and look at him—oh dear, what shall we do?" she whimpered distractedly.

"I'll just—" She shut the door. Feeling queerly abashed and ashamed of himself, Biørn got up, lit the lamp, and put on the most necessary clothes.

The child was in a high fever. His breath wheezed in his chest as he fought for it, and although his eyes were half open, he seemed unconscious of anything around him.

Miss Smith-Tellefsen sat on the edge of her bed and leaned over the boy's.

"Bikku darling—what's the matter with our little Bikku? Is it *so* bad? Look at me, Bikku—it's Åsta—what can we do for little Bikku, then?"

"Come come, Miss Tellefsen. It may not be anything much. Small children often run temperatures, you know. I expect it's just a chill. Let's pick him up, so that he can breathe more easily." Biørn wrapped the blanket round the little boy and took him in his arms.

"There we are, Bikku. Here's daddy. Don't you know your daddy? There! Feeling bad, are you? What's the idea of going sick, eh, son?"

Bikku whimpered something through his teeth, uttered a little frightened scream or two and reached out for Miss Tellefsen. She ran forward, threw herself over Bikku and kissed him where he lay in his father's arms.

"Yes, yes, Bikku—here I am! Here's Åsta—no, nobody's going to take you away—we'll look after you and make you better. There, sh—sh. Oh, Mr. Biørn, what *are* we to do? We must telephone for the doctor—let's send for him at once—*please!*"

"Let's wait and see, shall we? If it's just a severe chill we can't ask the doctor to come up here into the wilds in the middle of the night."

She threw herself into a chair and sobbed.

"O, dear God, help us—help us, God!"

Bikku suddenly bent double in a violent struggle for breath. It was dreadful to hear him. Miss Smith-Tellefsen shrieked at the top of her voice.

"He's dying! Think of your child, Mr. Biørn—you must, you must! Supposing it's pneumonia or diphtheria! Ring up the doctor, do! I can't—I shall go mad if I lose Bikku."

"Miss Tellefsen, *please!* Don't get so hysterical."

Still with the boy in his arms, he bent and put his arm round her waist to lift her up. But he withdrew his hand: she had no stays on, only a nightgown under her dress.

"Very well, I'll telephone, just to be on the safe side. Now you must please calm yourself—" for she had sprung up and grasped his arms.

He swore as he ran up the road in the wind and darkness. It was a six or seven-minute walk to the office; he had had the private telephone removed from his house because the workmen had taken to using it on Sundays and holidays.

When he returned, Miss Smith-Tellefsen was not in her room. She had laid the child in her own bed and propped him up with pillows. Biørn sat down on the edge of the bed.

Bikku looked really bad. If he were to lose him . . . For a moment he tried to imagine it. That, on top of all the rest: the crushing loneliness, the longing for his wife—that consuming, agonizing longing; a longing confused and clouded at times by a craving just for a woman—any woman. The horror that had forced itself upon him out there in the darkness, the empty office where he had called for help to people ten miles down the valley. It was then it had struck him that Bikku might be dying. The sense of helplessness which sickness brought with it up here— he remembered it from the last days of Borghild's life.

The room seemed so snug and quiet and cosy. Even bedroom air had a soothing, reassuring effect on him at that moment.

Miss Smith-Tellefsen came back with a bottle.

"What did the doctor say?"

"He wasn't in. I spoke to his wife. He'll come as soon as posible. I'm glad I telephoned, now."

Miss Smith-Tellefsen sighed.

"Oh, let's hope he comes soon. I thought perhaps a little cranberry juice in water might quench his thirst." She mixed it in a glass and tried to give it to Bikku, but most of it ran down his chin, onto his nightshirt and the pillow.

Miss Smith-Tellefsen began to cry, quite quietly, as she wiped it up and turned the pillow.

"Oh, dear God, what's going to happen—"

She sank hopelessly on to a chair by the head of the bed, rocking herself back and forth and weeping softly.

Biørn rose, went over to her, and laid his hand on her shoulder.

"Now please, my dear Miss Smith-Tellefsen! We don't *know* it's serious. You really must pull yourself together. It's worse for me, remember; I'm the boy's father."

She looked up helplessly. Her gentle brown eyes with the heavy pouches under them were brimming with tears.

"I love him so, Mr. Biørn—oh, I love him so."

Biørn suddenly stroked her cheek. And he went on, as if involuntarily, stroking and patting—until abruptly he took his hand away. He had come near the scars.

Bikku grew worse as the night went on, and his fever rose. Toward morning he had a terrible fit of coughing. Biørn, who had gone back to bed, rushed in cold with dread; never in his life had he heard anything like it. The child seemed to be coughing the very life out of his body with every paroxysm. But Miss Tellefsen was fairly steady and controlled now. She had remembered hearing about the use of the steam kettle in such cases, and the opportunity to do something practical had a calming effect upon her.

Later in the morning the doctor arrived, just in time to save the boy's life. For it was diphtheria, and an operation was necessary. Then Bikku was isolated with Miss Smith-Tellefsen and Serianna, while Laila and little Biørn were sent to Øifjell and their father moved into the office building.

2

HARDLY was Bikku well again, the house disinfected, and the household back to its normal routine when the engineer received a letter from a second cousin of his, inviting herself for a holiday.

This was Mrs. Hansen, a childless widow whose early marriage had lasted only a year. For many years since then she had worked as bookkeeper in a factory.

Mrs. Hansen was what people called "a jolly good sort." It was written all over her square face framed by curly blonde hair, her red-and-white, almost scrubbed-looking skin, and her pale-blue narrowed eyes that were always smiling between pale lashes. Her mouth was large and her teeth were splendid— and there seemed to be at least forty-eight of them, faultless and dazzling, when she laughed. And she laughed long and heartily: ha ha ha, with a clear, open a. She was tall and square and flat, held herself as straight as a soldier, and walked with long, firm steps. Every movement of hers proclaimed what a terribly good sort she was.

She came marching up to the verandah steps one evening, in brown *beksøm* boots, looped-up skirt, and a light shirt with a soft collar and tie. She carried a rucksack with jackets and a sweater dangling from it, and had a heavy hedge stake in her hand. There she stood, yodeling and shouting, until Miss Smith-Tellefsen appeared on the steps.

"Good evening. I'm Mrs. Hansen. Is my cousin at home? I suppose you're the housekeeper, aren't you? How do you do. Well, here I am!" She bared her teeth and held out her hand.

"How do you do, Mrs. Hansen." Miss Smith-

Tellefsen walked down the steps and surrendered her own hand. The visitor grasped it firmly and flung it away.

"I don't suppose you expected me this evening. Hope it's not inconvenient."

"Oh, not at all. At least, your room's not ready yet. We thought you'd be staying at the hotel tonight. Mr. Biørn had arranged for you to be driven up here early tomorrow."

"Goodness, no—that ghastly, dingy place. I had enough of it after just a meal there. Ugh, I thought it smelled of bedbugs, and if there's one thing in the world I'm scared of it's bedbugs. So I thought I'd do better to come straight on."

"You don't mean you've walked all the way! Bless my soul, you *must* be tired."

"Oh, well—in the ordinary way, twelve miles is nothing to speak of. But I pounded along as hard as I could, you know, so as to get up here by daylight. And anyhow I didn't know exactly how far it was. I've taken just—" she looked at her watch "—just three and a half hours. Of course, I am a bit tired."

"Yes, yes, we'll get your room ready at once. How brave of you to walk about the country like that on your own."

"Brave! What on earth is there to be afraid of? I know they say there are bears in the forest, but it seemed to me it would be pretty extraordinary if one of 'em came roaming along just where I happened to be. Tramps? Nonsense, they're all cowards. No, I'm not afraid of dogs—what an absurd idea. I took this along, you see." She thumped her stick on the floor. "Why, here's Bikku! Come along and say how-do to Aunt Kari, then. Why, what's the matter with him—is he scared? Shame, Bikku! I hope you're not a cowardy-custard."

But Bikku stayed behind Miss Tellefsen and peeped out suspiciously.

"Go and say how do you do nicely to the lady, Bikku. Poor Bikku," said Åsta, stroking his hair. "He's not used to strangers."

"He looks rather peaky, for a mountain boy. Oh, but of course, he's been ill. By the way, the place has been disinfected, hasn't it? My cousin wrote—"

"Why of course it has," Miss Tellefsen laughed. "Now, about your luggage." She took the rucksack to carry it upstairs. "Have you arranged for it to be sent up, or shall I telephone?"

"Luggage!" Mrs. Hansen flung her laughter-door wide open. "You've got it in your hand! That's all there is. Why, my dear Miss Tellefsen, how much more did you think I wanted to tote along with me—just for three weeks?"

Miss Smith-Tellefsen couldn't stand her. Serianna was cross about her coming, too: Mrs. Hansen had to have endless hot water carried upstairs, morning and evening, and she demanded porridge for breakfast every day. Laila couldn't endure Aunt Kari either; every morning at breakfast she delivered a lecture on porridge—how delicious it was, and how wholesome and how the children ought to have it—ought to be made to eat it. And whenever they got up or went to bed she came in and talked about cleanliness and sponging-down. She had Biørn's bedroom, and Biørn slept in the office building.

Mrs. Hansen and Biørn were sitting at the breakfast table one morning, and Miss Tellefsen was packing lunch for them in their rucksacks. They were to visit the old mines at Vardefjell, then go on and have a look at the top, and take a little turn round by Horr-kjønni, as Mrs. Hansen put it. She was in tremendous form after a hot sponge-down at 6:30 that morning, followed by a bath in the pool in the stream below the house; now she gulped her coffee and ate hard bread and whey cheese until crumbs were scattered all over the cloth.

"And you'll have some cream porridge for us then, Miss Tellefsen, won't you, when we come home? With lots of butter? When I'm in the mountains I can eat butter by the ladleful. And if the porridge won't mix smoothly, all you have to do is to say the names of three bald men—did you know that? Ha ha!"

Miss Smith-Tellefsen didn't laugh. That old joke was probably the only thing Mrs. Hansen knew about cream porridge and how to make it. She had an insufferable way of sticking her nose into housekeeping matters and offering advice, although she knew no more about it than the cat. The way she kept harping on cloudberries was bad enough: how odd it was that there were no cloudberries to be found up here. As if it was Miss Smith-Tellefsen's fault that the bad weather in July had destroyed the cloudberry blossom all over these hills.

Mrs. Hansen stuffed the rest of the hard bread into her mouth, emptied her coffee cup and pointed at the rucksacks.

"Are they ready, Miss Tellefsen? We'll start then, shall we, Torolf?"

"The children will be ready in a moment," said Miss Tellefsen. "Laila and Biørn do so want to stand on the steps and wave good-by to Daddy."

Mrs. Hansen looked at her watch.

"A quarter past eight! I really don't think it's a good thing to let them lie so late in the mornings. If I were you, Torolf, I'd *insist* on their being down to breakfast by eight sharp. It's good for children to form the habit of getting up early and being punctual."

"Laila's having her holidays," said Miss Tellefsen. "And the others are so small—"

"It's when they *are* small that they must be trained in these things, or they'll never learn." Mrs. Hansen settled down again and poured herself another cup of coffee. "But you know, Miss Tellefsen, I do think you're too lenient with the children. I've often thought I ought to mention it. It does children no good to give in to them so much. It spoils them and makes them soft. Well, Bikku, for instance. Fancy a child looking like that when he lives up here in this glorious mountain air."

"You must remember, though, Mrs. Hansen, that he's just been very ill. And anyway he's a little delicate by nature."

"That's what I mean. That boy needs hardening. Systematically. He ought to be running about out of doors all day instead of hanging around the kitchen and passages in the draught—which is *far* more treacherous than fresh, clean wind. Plenty of clothes on, of course—but what if he *is* out in the rain or gets his feet a bit wet? Trust nature to see he comes to no harm. Nobody could catch cold up in this glorious air where there are no bacteria. He ought to have a dip in the pool in the stream every morning, and then be rolled in a thick blanket and rubbed really hard. After that, a big plate of hot porridge. Then you'd see what a fine, sturdy fellow he'd become."

Miss Smith-Tellefsen snorted. "I don't interfere with the way other people bring up their children.

But these were entrusted to me by Mr. Biørn, and I look after them as my common sense tells me. I'm not going to risk Bikku's life for the sake of any new-fangled ideas, Mrs. Hansen."

"But you must remember, Miss Tellefsen," said Mrs. Hansen with a slight sneer, "as you say, these aren't your children, and you should allow members of their family to offer a little advice now and then. You know how it is: the care of children doesn't come easily to a person who's had none of her own, and who starts to look after them a little late in life. And I believe all elderly unmarried ladies make the mistake of being too anxious about them, and keeping them in cotton wool. I know a cousin of mine, Magda —do you remember, Torolf—?"

"Yes, Mrs. Hansen." Åsta Smith-Tellefsen drew herself up. "I've had about as many children as you have, I fancy. And how much you know about these things I can't tell. But forgive me for saying frankly that it doesn't seem a great deal. Now, I've been look-ing after these children for over two years. Bikku I've had since the night he was born, and nursed him through his teething and now this diphtheria—looked after him and sat up with him single-handed. I can truly say I fought for that child's life—can't I, Mr. Biørn? I think you know I do only what I believe is best for Bikku."

"Yes, yes, of course. You know, Karen, Miss Tellefsen does her very best for the boy."

"Well, naturally. I'm only saying what I think. Please don't upset yourself so, Miss Tellefsen."

"Dip Bikku in the pool!" Miss Smith-Tellefsen snorted. And as the other two went out, she flung after Mrs. Hansen: "And I think it's wrong to force Laila to eat porridge when she dislikes it so."

"Leave it, leave it, dear," she said, when the children came in from the verandah and started resignedly on the porridge; and she removed their plates. "Bread and butter and whey cheese are just as good for you, I'm sure. Such nonsense!"

Mrs. Hansen said no more on the subject as she and Biørn walked over the moors in the sunshine. She chatted away about her experiences in Jotunheim and Nordmarka, on Hardangervidda, the Hemsedal mountains, and Lyseheien.

"Having a look at the top" took three hours after leaving Vardefjell mines. Biørn sweated and puffed rather heavily: he had put on weight during the last years and had grown unused to walking. But Karen was bursting with energy as she strode ahead in the brown *beksøm* boots up the long, gentle slope of the hillside.

They found a sheltered place under the topmost cairn. Biørn stretched himself full length on the carpet of bearberry while Karen took out the spirit lamp, poured water from two beer bottles into the kettle, and unpacked the food.

"Yes, once you get up here you're glad you came," Biørn remarked, looking out at the view. "In this weather the hills are all right."

"Oh, there's nothing like them!" Mrs. Hansen cried rapturously.

On every side the uplands lay bathed in sunshine, golden brown and streaked with the gray-yellow of moss below the scree of lesser peaks, with green pasture land and bright osier beds along the streams and round the still, shining tarns. There was no trace of humanity to be seen, for the abandoned mines by Elsjø were hidden in a dip. Only opposite, on fenland under some low, black crags beyond the water, a few russet-colored dots were stirring, and the soft yet distinct ring of cowbells reached their ears. Above these boundless wastes, the sky arched clear and blue, dotted with little white clouds.

"Oh, I love the mountains," said Karen. "You know, Torolf, I'd like to live up here for the rest of my life."

"It's all very well in summer, but you don't know what it's like in autumn and winter—and right on until late spring. Ugh." He shrugged himself deeper into the bed of heath.

"How can you talk like that, Torolf? The hills are

glorious in all weathers. When I remember my last Easter trip—"

Biørn could not repress a little smile, but he said nothing, and Karen repeated: "Oh, the hills, the hills. I *love* the hills."

"Torolf," she said suddenly. "That housekeeper of yours—she's dug herself in rather firmly, hasn't she?"

He started.

"What do you mean?"

"Seems to me she lords it a bit—just as if it were her own house and her own children."

"She's bound to if she's to have any authority over the children. They must obey her, you know." He was silent for a time, and then went on: "She is good with them, there's no doubt. She was marvelous with Bikku when he had diphtheria. I couldn't help; I had to move out to the office. I couldn't risk spreading the infection. There are quite a lot of children in the miners' quarters, and an epidemic up here would have been no joke."

"In that case you can't know how marvelous she was. She wouldn't be likely to underrate what she did."

"Oh, yes, I do. Serianna knows all about it; she said she couldn't think how anyone could endure it like that. She adores Bikku. At first, when we realized how bad he was, she was nearly out of her mind— quite hysterical."

"These old maids easily get hysterical," observed Mrs. Hansen. Presently she laughed. "I wonder whether she isn't living in hopes, Torolf!"

Biørn made no answer.

"You be careful!" she went on playfully. "It's dangerous, my boy. Widower and housekeeper—ho ho!"

He lay pulling at the heather. Suddenly he said: "That's horribly true. It's not easy, you know—by God it's not!"

She glanced at him sharply.

"I know one thing. I could never love anyone else, after Borghild. Never, never have I been unfaithful to her in my heart, and I never will; I'm sure of that. But there's this about it, you see," he went on in a low voice. "I'm a strong, healthy man in the prime of life, with—with all the passions and instincts of a man. . . .

"No, it's not easy. I've been a widower for two years now, Karen. And all that time I've been alone up here in the wilds with a female person—seeing her every day, having all my meals with her, sleeping every night with only a door between us."

"Of course. You mustn't think I don't understand, Torolf," Mrs. Hansen said eagerly, bending over him with a warm and confidential air. She conveyed interest and intimacy in doing this, and for a moment Biørn regretted having spoken.

"Poor boy, I understand so well. I've often thought

about you and wondered how you were getting on up here. I know myself what it is to be alone—well, of course, it's not the same for a woman, but, having been married, one can understand something of it—and then the sorrow and the emptiness—oh, I *know!*"

Biørn lay staring out across the country, and presently as if involuntarily he continued: "No. I loved Borghild. One looks at things differently after a marriage like that. I was no saint in my bachelor days—never pretended to be—but now . . . Last winter there was a Swedish slut here—the wife of one of the miners, *she* said, but I'll never believe that. Ugh, what a creature—I can't bear to think of her.

"But Borghild—all that's over. That's what's so frightful—it's irrevocably over, and I know that nothing like it can ever come again. And frankly, I'm no good at living without a woman."

"So it might as well be this one as any other, you mean? Yes, I can see that. And she's kind, and she knows the house. And you've only to ask her—that's plain to see. Poor thing; it's only natural she should want to get married. Don't they all?"

"No, there's nothing wrong with it from that point of view. It's simply that she drives me mad—raving mad—by her perpetual smirk, and the way she trails after me, and that irritating chatter—it never stops."

"It's a pity she's so plain," said Mrs. Hansen.

"When I think of those scars—" He shuddered.

"Do you know, I almost think that moustache is the worst thing. Haven't you noticed it? No, that's true, she's very fair. I don't know anything so hopelessly unattractive as old maid's beard."

"When I imagine being married to her, sharing a room with her—and she'd be as loving as hell, too!" he said with a sudden, brutal laugh.

"Yes, they always are, old things like that who get married at the last moment," Karen agreed, laughing too.

"Brrr! No. And I'm sure she's terribly proper. If we have any trouble there, I shall simply have to marry her.

"And that's the damnable thing, you see—especially lately. I don't know how it happened, but now and again I've found myself putting a hand on her—playfully, really. God knows—perhaps she takes that as a beginning."

"I suppose nothing's happened to bind you in any way. I don't mean that you actually—I mean have you said or done anything to prevent your sliding out of it?"

"No," he said firmly. "Certainly not."

"I'll tell you what I think, Torolf. You should marry again, as soon as possible.

"You could marry her, of course. She has many good points. On the other hand, she has no interests —or none that I could discover. House, children, and cooking—above all cooking. So it would be simply having her as housekeeper plus. Well, wouldn't it? So I think you ought to try and find a nice, well-educated person who would be a companion to you— whom you could confide in—who would share your interests; play for you in the evenings and sometimes go with you on your trips, and so on. A sensible person, of course, who wouldn't expect you to sigh and languish and play the lover; a healthy, intelligent, decent person who would respect your sorrow and your memories, and be a good friend to you and a mother to your children."

"Not easy to find anyone like that, Karen." He laughed wearily. "No, poor old Åsta—I know where I am with her."

"Be careful, now, Torolf. I think you ought to arrange things so that when you go to Christiania at the end of the month you're able to stay there for a bit —refresh your mind, meet old friends, and so on. I'm sure you must know plenty of jolly girls from the old days. I'll do what I can to help, and arrange for you to meet the ones I think might be your kind."

But it proved unnecessary for Biørn to go bride-hunting in Christiania. The confidential talk with Mrs. Hansen was the first of many, so that by the time she left everything was settled. Biørn returned from Christiania wearing a new engagement ring next his old one, and he broke the news to his children and Miss Smith-Tellefsen. The wedding was to be at Christmas, and Miss Smith-Tellefsen was to stay on until the New Year, when the newly married couple would come home and the young wife take over the housekeeping.

3

BIØRN was rather sorry for Miss Smith-Tellefsen. She studied the advertisements in the *Aftenposten* every single day, wrote applications and posted them, but never had a reply. And he was touched by the way she had taken his news, for he realized that his engagement and her coming departure were a blow to her. But she toiled away gallantly, bottling and salting and making jam more diligently than ever before: "So much pleasanter for your wife to come to a well-stocked house. Otherwise the poor lady might find things a little difficult in the beginning, you know."

When Biørn first came back from Christiania, he was tremendously excited. He looked forward with longing to the end of his widowerhood and was greatly impressed by his fiancée. She had known so well how to salve his conscience with regard to his first wife and had spoken gently and sympathetically of Biørn's and Borghild's love for each other. Between Biørn and Karen there was of course no question of anything like that. They were fond of each other in quite a different way; they would be friends and companions: "Your best friend, Torolf, whom you can confide in—a steadfast, reliable, loyal friend." She talked of bringing her piano; she prophesied idyllic evenings of music and cards, and glorious mountain walks; and she had the wholesomest, most moral ideas about the upbringing of children. The only thing Biørn didn't quite like—though he wouldn't admit it even to himself—was that she too emphasized her continued fidelity to the late Mr. Hansen, in spite of the new kind of love and the new marriage.

During the blissful early days of his betrothal, Biørn was very amiable to Miss Smith-Tellefsen, and had talked to her more freely and openly than usual. Once or twice, despite the fiancée in Christiania and the approaching conjugal paradise, he even touched her, he hardly knew how or why.

He passed it off with a joke, of course, but secretly he was both alarmed and distressed. The old Adam in him, it seemed, was not content with the prospect of entering the promised land at Christmas; on the contrary, Biørn did not know how he was going to get through the next three months. The more he pictured to himself how heavenly everything would be when he brought Karen up here, with her piano and books and interests and so forth, the more hopeless those months appeared.

Then the autumn gales burst over the mountains, putting an end to his shooting and keeping him in-doors. He stayed in his office as much as possible and went to bed early—not always a good thing, he found —nevertheless he could not avoid being more in her company than usual during this time. And in his frame of mind, Miss Smith-Tellefsen became an al-luring, menacing danger.

At the end of September the weather suddenly turned brilliantly sunny and still, and quite abnormally warm for the time of year.

The engineer's house was surrounded by a piece of fenced ground known as the garden. Only heather and dwarf birch grew right by the house, amid patches of bare rock, but farther down, where the hill began to slope toward the valley, there were a few fir trees; and grass, mountain flowers, and silver-gray osiers grew luxuriantly along the stream. Just above the pool, in a sort of cave, benches and a table had been placed, and Miss Smith-Tellefsen had planted some rhubarb as an experiment.

On Sunday, which was the last day of September, the weather was like that of midsummer. Miss Tellef-sen and Biørn had coffee in the cave. They were alone, for the children had gone off to Øifjell to watch the milking.

"It's wonderful here now," Miss Tellefsen said,

looking over the russet moorland opposite and the blue-green valley below. "When I think what it was like only last week—!"

"Yes, it's lovely this evening," said the engineer.

"Oh, how I shall miss this place and long to be here again." She sighed.

"Well, let's hope you'll be able to find something a little livelier. It must often have been pretty dreary for you here, I should think."

"A little lonely, perhaps, now and then." She was silent for a while. Her voice had grown unsteady. "But it's been such a home, you see. And that won't be easy to find anywhere else." She had to pause again. "I'd like best to be on a farm in the country—if possible where there was no mistress of the house. Then perhaps I could invite the children to visit me. You must let them come, Mr. Biørn. It would seem so strange not to see them any more."

She raised her moist, brown, dog's eyes to his. And it dawned on Biørn that she had done much more for the children than anyone had a right to expect of a paid housekeeper, and that it must be painful for her to leave them. He put down his whisky glass, went over to her, and took her hand.

"Of course I will. I know I can never thank you enough for all you've done for my poor children."

She clutched his hand convulsively.

"I'm really dreading having to leave them—" and

suddenly she broke down. She bowed over the stone table in bitter weeping.

"Please, my dear Miss Tellefsen—" An idea occurred to him, and in his pleasure at this he sat down beside her on the bench and tried to raise her head.

"You know you can always look on this place as a home, Miss Tellefsen. You must come up and visit us on your holidays, naturally."

"Oh, no!" She wept quietly on the table. "Oh, no—"

As she lay thus, a line of gleaming white skin showed between the red silk blouse and the black scarf. Biørn couldn't take his eyes off it as he bent lower and lower over her; his hand approached it once or twice as he asked: "But why not? My dear, why ever not? Why shouldn't you come and see me?"

For a moment she looked up, dazed and bewildered. When he kissed her, she never thought of resisting; she sank against him and lay in his arms, soft and heavy and hot, and let him do as he would. And when Biørn came to himself and released her, she remained half lying on the bench, staring blankly up at him.

He was trembling all over. This time, by God, it had been touch and go.

Åsta stretched up her arms to him.

"Do you care for me then, after all?"

"God help us, I think we're both out of our minds," he whispered, horror-stricken.

1 8 9

Slowly she stood up. Then suddenly the lament burst from her: "I care for you much, much more than she does. And then the children—think of the children—"

"Hush, for goodness' sake—" He spoke in the same scared whisper as before. "Don't scream like that. You know perfectly well—" then he turned suddenly and walked—almost ran—back to the house.

At supper they exchanged not a word. Biørn was desperately ill at ease. On the few occasions when their eyes met, she looked at him in such a helpless, miserable, inquiring way—phew!

Afterwards he went straight upstairs. Anything to avoid having it out this evening and hearing her cry all night. And when she came up, he lay listening, tensely. *Was* she crying?

Next morning at breakfast he told her he was going over to Blåfjell for a week. She simply nodded.

When they had finished the meal he had to say it: "Miss Smith-Tellefsen, may I have a word with you?" They stood opposite one another, alone in the big, bare sitting-room with its shiny oiled paneling. Biørn looked down.

"Well now, Miss Tellefsen—you'll understand. . . . Of course you shall be paid right up to the New Year. But it would be best if you left now, at once. As soon as you can be ready."

"Yes, I quite understand, Mr. Biørn. I shall be gone by the time you get back from Blåfjell."

"Yes." He sighed with relief. "That's the wisest thing. I'm sure you realize that yourself."

"I'll say good-by now, then, Miss Smith-Tellefsen." He went to her and pressed her hand. "The very best of luck to you, and I hope you'll be happy in your new place. Thank you for all you've done for me and the children—many, many thanks."

"And thank you." She lifted her tear-bright eyes and looked into his. There was a strange light over her elderly face. "I shall be glad to go now. I can see it must be so. I can go, now that I know you care for me."

He bent his head and was silent. She went to the door. But then suddenly she turned and broke out again in that queer, moaning voice: "Say it just once —tell me just once that you love me! Won't you kiss me—just once—before I go?"

Painfully disconcerted and embarrassed he answered: "My dear Miss Smith-Tellefsen, please— please be sensible. I know I've behaved badly, but I never meant to—you must see that. I ought to have had more self-control, I admit. But, good God, it's not easy for two people thrown together as we've been, alone up here in the wilds. Surely you understand that—damn it, you're not a youngster any more—"

She didn't look as if she'd understood; she simply

stared, dazed and despairing. And the shame he felt made him furious and brutal.

"—and don't try to tell me you don't know about these things. Seems to me you had a pretty good idea of what you wanted from me. I confess I've behaved badly," he added in a subdued tone; then, seemingly on the verge of flaring up again: "But you must admit you're to blame too."

Miss Smith-Tellefsen burst into tears. She said nothing; she merely sobbed. But when he approached her she fled from the room.

When Biørn returned from Blåfjell, Miss Smith-Tellefsen and all her belongings had disappeared.

4

For a month Åsta Smith-Tellefsen stayed in a cheap pension and looked for a situation. At last she decided on one with a religious-minded widow who was seeking a practicing Christian as companion-help. Indeed, this was the only place she had been able to find, and if she had waited any longer she would have had to break into her savings.

The situation was not exactly what Miss Smith-Tellefsen had been looking for. The salary was only eighteen crowns a month, and no maid was kept. But a woman came in to wash the clothes; the lady had her wood and coal delivered regularly in small quantities, so Miss Tellefsen wouldn't have to carry that upstairs, and the outside staircase had to be washed no more than once a week, as there were two flats to a landing. There were only three rooms; the courtyard was quiet; there were no children, and it was a good neighborhood. There would be just the two of them, so all in all it was a fairly pleasant, easy place.

The religious-minded lady was the widow of a well-to-do saddler named Johansen. She was quite nice, poor thing, thought Miss Smith-Tellefsen. But it was very quiet there: nobody came to the place except a few elderly ladies. Mrs. Johansen had told Åsta that a number of pastors and theologians would be coming in and out, but Miss Smith-Tellefsen saw nothing of them. On the other hand, Mrs. Johansen attended a great many meetings and sewing-clubs and missions and bazaars and the like. Her passion was the clergy: knowing clergymen and talking to and about clergymen. A niece of hers, the daughter of the late Mr. Johansen's sister, was married to a clergyman, but they lived such a long way away in the north that they existed only as a topic of conversation.

Åsta had the Storakers to talk about, as she sat sewing with Mrs. Johansen in the sitting-room. And talk about them she did; it was such a joy to recall them and old pastor Hellesnaes their predecessor, and the prayer meetings at Høgste, and everything about those hills and valleys. It was a comfortable sitting-room, with texts in silver lettering on black cards, and religious pictures, and portraits of pastors wherever one looked. It faced Bogstad Road, which was a fairly lively street with a good deal of traffic. Her own room —the maid's—faced the courtyard and was small and dark, so that her belongings had to be crowded together. But she was in it only at night, and when the lamp was lit it was really quite snug.

On the little table in front of the window stood the photographs of Biørn's children, taken at the Storakers' house by a traveling photographer. There was a group of all three, and a picture of herself with Bikku in her arms.

She cried a little every night over these photographs. For hours she would lie in bed with the lamp burning, just thinking of all that had happened in the engineer's house. And the tears fell; gentle, melancholy tears.

The memory of saying good-by to the children cut her to the heart. Yet it was some consolation to remember how Laila grieved at her leaving, and how sweet and good she had been toward the end. Poor little soul, no doubt she was dreading her new stepmother. Her behavior to Miss Smith-Tellefsen, from the moment her father had broken the news to her, had altered beyond recognition.

The last scene between herself and Biørn, which

she had not quite understood, recurred to her over and over again; she erased the recollection and altered it until she could weep gentle tears over that too. She tried to comfort herself for the slightly bitter taste of it—for this she could never altogether lose—by recalling something that had been said to her by an elderly and experienced housekeeper at her very first place: men had frightfully strong passions, but the poor fellows couldn't help it.

At last one day the widow was to give a party. The guests were to be a young chaplain, two theologians, a religious-minded clockmaker and his wife, and the ladies who always came to visit Mrs. Johansen.

Åsta Smith-Tellefsen was really looking forward to seeing some new faces. When she brought in the chocolate and cakes she was wearing her red blouse with a big new neck scarf. But disappointment awaited her. Mrs. Johansen never introduced her, and there was no room for her at the table, so that she was left sitting forlornly in the corner by the window. Not until she had cleared away the chocolate and brought in the coffee did one of the theologians—the one who had said grace—come over to her.

"I haven't had the pleasure of meeting you before, I believe. My name is Høibraaten."

He was a remarkably handsome young man, with yellow hair as curly as a fleece, and bright-blue eyes.

And he was most interesting to talk to. In many respects he followed the new trends in divinity, he told
her. They were in the middle of an animated conversation, and Åsta was smiling and gay, when
Mrs. Johansen called to her to clear away the coffee
things.

Mrs. Johansen came into the kitchen when she was
taking the cups off the tray.

"I think it would be best if you washed up now, at
once, Miss Tellefsen. I'm rather afraid of leaving
those good cups out. And—" she hesitated. "I wanted
to ask you to wear another blouse. That one looks so
worldly, somehow."

Åsta's face was crimson.

"Then when you're ready you can come in again.
We're going to have a little service before supper."

Miss Smith-Tellefsen's tears dripped steadily into the
washing-up water. She hardly knew why she felt so
hopelessly poor and humiliated and forsaken, or why
she wept so despairingly in her room, as she changed
into her high-necked black blouse.

SIMONSEN

SIMONSEN stopped in the gateway and dug out his worn, greasy old wallet, meaning to slip into it the testimonial he had in his hand. But first he unfolded the grimy paper and read it through, although he knew it by heart:

"Storeman Anton Simonsen has been with our firm for three years. During this time he has shown himself to be a sober, hard-working, and willing man.

N. Nielsen
Hercules Engineering Works."

No, indeed; that reference wouldn't do him much good. Damn the fellow, it was a shabby way to treat him. The chief had never minded pitching the tale to customers about delivery dates and things like that— but write the sort of reference that would get a poor devil a job—not likely! "Well, I can't state that you've carried out your work to our satisfaction," he'd said, the so-and-so. But at least he'd had to put "sober." He hadn't at first, but Simonsen had insisted. "Seems to me I've smelled drink *on* you from time to time, Simonsen." But Simonsen had spoken up. "I do take a nip now and again, sir," he'd said. "And I believe you would too, if you had to spend your days rummaging about in that cold warehouse. But nobody can say Anton Simonsen was ever the worse for drink at his work—no, not even tipsy. Not once." So then his lordship had to give in and the secretary lady had to write it out again with "sober" in it. And now here it was—such as it was; no great shakes, but he had nothing better to show.

"Look out, blast you—fathead!"

Simonsen jumped aside against the wall as a cartload of clattering iron girders swung into the gateway. Steam rose from the horses' damp backs as they threw themselves into the collar to drag the sleigh over the bare paving-stones under the arch. The driver shouted something else after him, but Simonsen couldn't hear it for the din of the clashing girders.

He put away his testimonial and slipped the wallet into his breast pocket. Then he glanced indignantly after the sleigh. It was standing in the yard in front of the warehouse, under the crane which projected with its chain and pulley from a dark hole above the barred windows in the blackish-red wall. White steam was rising from the horses' backs, and their coats were matted into little wet, frosty tufts. The carter hadn't put their rugs on them; he was talking to another man.

Simonsen buttoned up his winter overcoat, which was fairly new and tidy, straightened himself up, and threw out his stomach. A sense of his dignity as a citizen arose in him; he was, after all, a respectable member of society, and that ruffian of a driver had bawled at him. And with this feeling something else stirred within him at the sight of the two cart horses, which had hauled their load until the muscles of their sweating loins were tense. He stepped back into the yard.

"You ought to cover those horses of yours, you know. Why d'you let 'em stand in the cold like that, in a muck sweat?"

The carter—a tall lout of a fellow—turned and looked down at him.

"Is that any o' your business, fellow?"

"They'd have something to say to you, wouldn't they, if I was to go up to the office and tell 'em how you treat their animals?"

"Just you get out—and quick about it! What the hell's it got to do with you, eh? Shoving your nose in—" and he took a step toward Simonsen.

Simonsen withdrew a little—but of course the fellow would never dare touch him here in the yard. He stuck out his stomach even farther, saying: "Don't forget they can see you from the office windows, that's all —see how you look after the firm's horses."

With that he turned. And at once the feeling of

self-confidence ebbed away. For as he was passing through the gateway a man ran down the steps and shot past him, a gentleman, wearing an astrakhan cap and a fur coat, and carrying a black stick with a silver handle—a red-and-white, fair-haired man, the man he had spoken to when he applied for the job.

Dusk was falling. It was nearly four o'clock. Olga would have something to say about it when he arrived back so late for dinner. Well, he'd just have to tell her he'd been kept late at the warehouse.

Simonsen padded quickly along Torv Street. He both shuffled and hopped, and with his big round belly and little curved arms he looked rather like a rubber ball rolling and bouncing along. He was a little, short-necked man with a pouchy, fat face and watery eyes hidden far in behind their lids, red-veined cheeks, and a rather blue blob of a nose above the bristly, grayish-yellow moustache.

It was a raw Saturday afternoon early in December, and the air was thick with gray frost-fog that smelled and tasted of gas and soot. Out in the street the sleighs swung from side to side over the ploughed-up, pot-holed, hard-frozen snow, while on the pavement the stream of people flowed black and heavy past the il-luminated, frosted shopwindows. Somebody bumped into Simonsen every moment, and looked back at him angrily as he bumbled along deep in his own thoughts.

Not that many thoughts were stirring in his mind,

for he thrust them away. He'd find something, some-how, somewhere. So he needn't tell Olga that he'd been sacked at last, and was to leave on New Year's Day. Heigh-ho—the battle of life.

There was no great hurry. He had nearly a month. But if it came to the pinch, he'd have to write to Sigurd. Sigurd would always be able to find him a job. It wasn't too much to ask of one's own son—when the son was in Sigurd's position. Still, he didn't care for the idea; it would be for the fourth time. The fourth time in eight whole years, though—eight years exactly at the New Year, since Sigurd had got him into the office because his smart new daughter-in-law, the bitch, didn't think he was good enough to live with them in Fredrikstad. It was a pity he'd lost all three jobs—but that wasn't his fault. At the office it was the girls who'd done for him, cheeky little sluts. As if it mattered to them what he was like so long as he did his work properly—and he had. And he'd taken no liberties with them—as if he would, with such stuck-up, white-faced shrews. And then there was the timber yard. In those days he'd been really neat and respectable, for it was then he had moved to Olga's. He wasn't used to that sort of job, of course; but if it hadn't been for the foreman's malice he would never have lost it. And then he was taken on by the engineering works. And what sort of situation was that for a man nearing sixty, having to learn about a whole lot of queer new things he'd never heard of, and dispatching and packing and invoicing and all the rest of it. The chief storeman was a lazy devil; Simonsen was blamed for everything, and they'd always treated him badly—all of them, from the manager and the chief clerk (who kept reminding him that he'd only been taken on temporarily and asking him whether he had anything else in view) to the head storeman and the foreman and the drivers—*and* the cashier: how sour and cross she'd been every time he went up to her to ask for an advance!

All these things went round and round in his head, rolled up in a gray, woolly fog of anxiety and depression: Olga would nag at him when he got home, Sigurd and his wife would make themselves most unpleasant when they heard he'd been dismissed, and he would have to make a fresh start in a new job where he would dither, frightened and uncomprehending and woolly-minded, faced with new work that he knew nothing about and would never learn, in a new warehouse or perhaps a new office full of strange, hostile things, cowering under constant correction and rebuke, dully awaiting a fresh dismissal—just as he had dithered and cowered, heavy and old and stupid, through his previous situations.

But Simonsen had had a certain amount of practice in keeping gloomy thoughts at bay. He had dithered through his whole life in just the same way; he had cowered and expected dismissal and reprimand and nagging and unpleasantness as something inevitable. So it had been at sea, so it had been on Consul Isachsen's wharf, and so it had been at home while his wife was alive. She had been ill-tempered and sour and strict and cross-grained—and his daughter-in-law was not so very different.

Yes, Sigurd had been paid out for marrying that shabby-genteel daughter of Captain Myhre's. What good times Simonsen had had at home after Laura's death! The boy had come on well: he'd been good to his old dad—paid his way and everything. Not that it had been so bad here in town either, for the first few years, when he'd been a gay bachelor again, going out and about and having fun. And since he'd taken up with Olga he'd really been very comfortable—on the whole. She hadn't been too easy the time she became pregnant, but that was understandable, and she had calmed down the moment he promised to marry her. Sometimes she went on at him to keep his word, and of course he fully intended to marry her sometime; he'd have done it long ago if he hadn't known what trouble he'd have over it with Sigurd and his wife. But one day he'd find a good, easy job that he could keep, and when Olga expanded her dress-making business, and her boy Henry went into the office—he was errand-boy there now, and shaping well—they would all be happy and comfortable together. He would sit on the sofa with his toddy and his pipe, and Olga would flit in and out seeing to things, and Svanhild would sit beside him and do her homework. For Olga was a decent, steady person, and nobody should have a chance to call Svanhild a bastard when she started school.

Simonsen had reached Ruseløk Road. The fog lay heavy and raw in the narrow street, and was barred with light—yellowish-green light from the frozen panes of the little shopwindows. In all of these, visible where gas jet or lamp had thawed a clear patch, hung a cluster of paper Christmas-tree baskets, whether it was a draper's or a delicatessen store or a tobacco shop. The reddish glow from the big windows of the market hall on the other side of the street flowed oilily out into the fog; the gas lamps on the terrace above could just be glimpsed, but the big private houses up there were invisible; not a gleam of light came from them, though one could sense them like a wall high up in the fog, pressing down upon the street that ran like a ditch at their foot.

Simonsen toddled and trudged along; the pavement was slippery in many places where the sheet-ice had not been chipped away. Children swarmed in and out of the dark gateways, and in the street among carts and sleighs they tried to slide, wherever there

was as much as a slippery runner-track through the
bumpy, brown layer of hard-frozen snow.

"Svanhild!"

Simonsen called sharply to a little girl in a dirty
white hood. She had clambered up on to the piled-up
snow along the edge of the pavement, and from there
slid down to the roadway on tiny skis that were black
with dirty snow and had hardly any curve left in
them.

The child stood still in the middle of the street,
looking up at Simonsen, who had stepped over the
heap of snow to her. Her blue eyes were conscience-
stricken, as she brushed her fair hair up under her
hood and wiped her nose on her red-mittened hand.

"How many times have you been told not to run
out into the street, Svanhild! Why can't you be a good
girl and play in the yard?"

Svanhild looked up fearfully.

"I can't ski in the yard; there isn't any slope."

"And suppose a cart came along and ran over you
—or a drunken man carried you off—what d'you
think Mum and Dad would say then, eh?"

Svanhild, ashamed, was silent. Simonsen helped her
on to the pavement, and they tripped along together
hand in hand, her little sticks of skis clattering on the
snowless path.

"Do you think Dad'll take you for a walk this evening, when you're such a naughty, disobedient girl, and don't do what you're told? Finished dinner, I suppose, have they?"

"Mummy and Henry and me had dinner a long time ago."

"H'm." Simonsen trudged in through the gateway. MRS. OLGA MARTINSEN. DRESSMAKING. CHILDREN'S AND BOYS' CLOTHES. 3rd FLOOR. ENTRANCE IN YARD was the legend on a white enamel plate. Simonsen crossed the courtyard and glanced up at the lighted window, where some fashion magazines were propped up against the panes. Then he took Svanhild's skis under his arm and led the child up the narrow stairs at the back of the yard.

Outside Olga's door some little boys were reading a comic by the light of a kitchen lamp that hung there. Simonsen growled something and let himself in.

It was dark in the hall. At the farther end, light shone through the glass pane in the sitting-room door. Simonsen went into his own room. It was dark in there too, and cold. Damn it, she'd let the stove go out. He lit the lamp.

"Run in to Mummy, Svanhild, and tell her I'm back."

He opened the door into the next room. At the table, which overflowed with half-finished sewing, pieces cut out and scraps left over, Miss Abrahamsen sat bowed over her work. She had fastened a newspaper to one side of the lamp, so that all the light fell upon her yellow little old-maid's face and brown, rat's paw hands. The steel of the two sewing-machines glinted a little, and against the wall Olga's and Svanhild's white-covered beds could just be discerned.

"Hard at it, then, Miss Abrahamsen!"

"Yes, well—you got to be."

"Funny, this Christmas business. You'd think the world was coming to an end."

Svanhild crept into the room.

"Mum says your dinner's in the oven."

"I shall sit here and enjoy your company, Miss Abrahamsen. It's cold in my room."

Miss Abrahamsen silently cleared a corner of the table while Simonsen fetched his meal: white cabbage soup and sausage.

H'm. Good. If only he'd had— Simonsen rose and knocked at the sitting-room door.

"I say, Olga—"

"Why, good evening, Mr. Simonsen! How are you keeping?"

He opened the door and looked in.

"So it's you! Another new dress, Miss Hellum?"

Olga was standing with her mouth full of pins, fitting her customer. She arranged the folds at Miss Hellum's breast, in front of the wall mirror.

"Like that, I thought." Olga took the lamp from the nickel stand beside her and held it up.

"Ye—es. You're sure its not lopsided at the back, now, Mrs. Martinsen?"

Two girls who were sitting and waiting in the half light over on the plush sofa put down a fashion journal, glanced at each other and smiled, looked at Miss Hellum and smiled at each other again. "Gracious!" one whispered audibly. They were dressed almost exactly alike, in three-quarter-length coats with a little strip of fur at the neck, and respectable felt hats trimmed with a bird's wing. Simonsen paused in the doorway; he was a little shy of them.

"What do you think of it, Mr. Simonsen? Is it going to look nice?"

"How well that color suits you, Miss Hellum! But to beauty all is becoming, as they say."

"Ah, go on with you!" Miss Hellum laughed. Pretty girl, that. Olga was cutting round the neck, and her customer bent her head a little and shivered at the touch of the cold scissors. She had a pretty, plump neck with curly yellow hair growing low on it, and soft round arms.

"I expect this costs a bit," said Simonsen, feeling the silk—and then feeling her arm, as Olga went to fetch the sleeve.

"Shame on you, Mr. Simonsen!" laughed Miss

Hellum. Olga looked annoyed; she shoved him aside and pulled on the sleeve.

"What was I going to say? . . . Oh, yes, Olga. Do you think Henry could nip down and borrow a couple of beers?"

"Poor Henry had to go back to the office; there was an estimate to be copied, he said."

"Oh, did he? Too bad. It's the same every Saturday evening nowadays, seems to me. Yes, it's a grind all right. And it was nearly four before I could get away from the warehouse. Oh, to be young and lovely, Miss Hellum!"

Svanhild looked in.

"Come along, Svanhild. Do you remember my name today?"

"Miss Hellum." Svanhild smiled obediently.

"Would you like some sweets again today?" Miss Hellum looked into her handbag and brought out a paper cornet.

"What do you say now, Svanhild? Your right hand, mind, and a pretty curtsy."

Svanhild whispered thank you, gave her right hand, and curtsied. Then she began breaking apart the camphor-drop sweets that had stuck together in the paper bag.

Miss Hellum dressed and talked and laughed.

"I'll be along for the final fitting on Tuesday, then,

at the same time. You won't let me down, Mrs. Martinsen, will you? Good-by, then. Good-by, Mr. Simonsen. 'Bye, Svanhild."

Simonsen gallantly opened the door for her, and she swept out with waving feathers, the muskrat stole flung stylishly back over her shoulder.

"Gosh," said one of the young girls on the sofa. "Not bad."

"Hee-hee! No, she's a one, all right."

Simonsen went back to Miss Abrahamsen and his dinner, which had grown cold. Olga came in soon afterwards, fetched the coffee, and poured it out.

"I don't understand you, Anton, playing the fool like that! What can you be thinking of—in front of other people, too."

"Who cares about those little baggages?"

"It was the pastor's daughter from the Terrace and her friend. You make things hard enough for me as it is, without carrying on so silly with Miss Hellum. Yes, that's given them something to talk about—as if they hadn't enough already!"

"Ah, go on—it wasn't as bad as that."

The front doorbell rang. Miss Abrahamsen went to answer it.

"It's Miss Larsen."

Olga put down her cup and laid a tacked-up dress over her arm.

"Never any peace—"

Miss Abrahamsen bent over her sewing again.

Mrs. Martinsen and Miss Abrahamsen sat sewing all that Sunday. They put off dinner until it was too dark to work; afterwards Olga lit the lamp and they started again.

"That plastron for Miss Olsen's dress, Miss Abrahamsen—you were working on it just now, weren't you?"

Miss Abrahamsen buzzed away at the machine.

"I put it on the table."

Olga searched, and looked about the floor.

"Svanhild, you haven't seen a little piece of white lace, have you?"

"No," said Svanhild from the window. She crept out and began searching too—but first she laid her doll on the upturned stool that was its bed, and covered it up well.

"Astrid's asleep—she's got diphtheria and scarlet fever," Svanhild protested, as her mother hunted through the doll's things. But relentlessly Olga lifted the patient—it was wrapped in white, ruched lace fastened carefully with safety pins.

"Good gracious! The child must be out of her mind! And I do declare you've torn a hole in it with the pins—you naughty, wicked girl—" she smacked her "—oh, what *shall* I do? Miss Olsen's expensive lace . . ."

Svanhild howled.

"Haven't I told you never to take anything that's on the floor? You're a wicked, mischievous little girl!"

Miss Abrahamsen inspected the plastron.

"I can unpick the pleats and press it and pleat it again so's to hide the tear in a fold. I don't think it'll show—"

Svanhild was yelling at the top of her voice. Simonsen opened the door a crack.

"What on earth's the matter, Svanhild—screaming like that when you know Daddy's taking his nap?"

Olga explained, vehemently.

"Oh, what a bad girl, Svanhild, to play such a nasty trick on your mother. You're not my Svanhild any more."

"I think you might take her out for a bit, Anton. It can't be good for you to lie in bed and sleep all day."

Simonsen scolded the child vigorously as he set off with her. But when they got as far as the hall and he helped her into her outdoor things, he comforted her.

"Don't cry any more now—oh, what an ugly noise! We'll go and toboggan in the Palace Park. It was very wrong of you, you know. Blow your nose now—there. You and I will go off and toboggan now—come along, Svanhild love."

Olga was really too strict with the child sometimes. Not that children shouldn't be punished when they did wrong—but Svanhild took things to heart so. There she was, still sobbing on the sled behind him—poor little mite.

The evening sky was dark purple above the towers and spires of the Terrace. The weather had cleared, and only a thin, sooty frost-haze hung in the streets round the lamps when Simonsen trudged uphill dragging his daughter on the sled.

It was so pretty in the park. Thick white hoarfrost lay on all the trees and bushes, so that they sparkled in the lamplight. But what crowds of children everywhere! On every smallest slope they were sledding or skiing; in the big avenue were swarms of big, rough boys, five or six of them on a fish sledge, yelling and shrieking as they whizzed down over the frozen snow with a long, thin rat's tail of sticks behind them. But Simonsen knew of a nice, quiet little slope; he and Svanhild had often tobogganed there in the evenings. It was fun for her there; Daddy stood at the top and gave her a shove, Svanhild shouted: "Way!" till her thin little voice nearly cracked, and Simonsen roared: "Way!" from right down in his stomach, although the only other people there were two little boys in ski-runners' shoes and woolen caps. Simonsen spoke to them; their names were Alf and Johannes Hauge, and their father was head of a government office and lived in Park Road. Simonsen gave all three children a shove—they were going to see whose sled ran fastest

—but he shoved Svanhild hardest so that she won. Then he trotted down after them and helped Svanhild up again, for otherwise her feet broke through the frozen crust of the snow and she got stuck.

But presently Svanhild began to whimper.

"Daddy, my feet are so cold."

"Run then, my dear—come along, we'll go up onto the path and run."

Svanhild ran and cried; her toes hurt her so.

"Come now, you must run faster than that—much, much faster, Svanhild. Try and catch me!"

Simonsen bounced along with little tiny steps, like a rubber ball. And Svanhild ran after him as hard as she could and caught him up—again and again until she was warm and cheerful again, and laughing.

But then they couldn't find the sled. Simonsen hunted above the slope and below the slope and in among the bushes, but it was gone. Alf and Johannes had seen it standing over by the big tree near the path a little while before, but that was all they knew. Yes, and some big, rough boys had passed—Simonsen remembered that. It must have been they who took it.

Svanhild cried bitterly. Simonsen thought of Olga —oh, she really ought to be kinder; she was so snappy all day. Nasty, bad boys to steal a poor little girl's sled. How could children be so cruel.

"Don't cry, sweetheart, we'll find it again, you'll see."

Simonsen trotted about from slope to slope asking if anyone had seen a little blue sled. Svanhild went with him, holding his hand and crying; Alf and Johannes came too, clutching their sled ropes as with wide eyes they told Simonsen all the dreadful things they had heard about big, nasty boys who stole sleds and tobogganed into little children and threw lumps of ice in the Palace Park.

There was no sign of the sled. And up in the main avenue they met a grand, angry lady who turned out to be Alf's and Johannes' nanny, and she scolded them for not having come in half an hour before, and promised them they would catch it from Mummy and Daddy. She wasn't a bit interested to hear that the little girl was called Svanhild and that she had lost her sled; she went on scolding and scolding as she shuffled away holding the little boys' hands in a nurse's iron grasp. And Simonsen nearly got a steering-stick in his eye and the tip of a sled on his shin.

"Well, I'm afraid they've taken your sled, Svanhild; I don't think we shall see *that* again." Simonsen sighed dejectedly. "Hush now, don't cry so, my darling. Daddy'll give you a fine new sled for Christmas. There! Come along, we'll go down Karl Johan and look at the shops—they're wonderful tonight—and perhaps we'll see a fine new sled for you there," he said, brightening.

So Svanhild and her daddy went and looked at the

shops. And when they came to a window where the crowds had halted and clustered in a big, black, jostling mass, Simonsen lifted her up on his arm and wriggled and shoved until they got right up to the shining window, and there they stood until there wasn't a single thing in it about which they hadn't talked and wondered how much it cost. In some places there were decorated Christmas trees with electric lights on their branches—and Svanhild was going to have a tree too, on Christmas Eve. In one shop there was a Christmas party, with tremendously grand lady dolls—just like Svanhild would be when she grew up. And in a shop where they sold trunks and suitcases, there was a tiny, tiny crocodile in a tiny, tiny pool; they had to wait a long time—could it be alive? And at last it blinked one eye the teeniest bit. Fancy, it *was* alive! A little crocodile like that would grow up to be so big that it could eat up a whole Svanhild at one gulp—"but this one can't bite, can it?" "No, this one couldn't do you any harm."

Up in Ekertorvet there was a movie camera in the window, among advertisements in photographs. And Svanhild had been to a movie with Daddy—three times—and they had to go over all they had seen there: the two little girls who had been kidnapped by kidnappers in a motor car, and a lot more. The lost sled was quite forgotten—and so was Mummy, sitting with pursed lips at her sewing until she grew tired and cross—everything was forgotten except that Svanhild was Daddy's little girl and that in seventeen days it would be Christmas.

There was a sports shop with sleds in the window, sleds large and small—but the finest of all, the scarlet one with rose-painting [1] on it and a bronzed iron back-rest—that was the one Daddy would give Svanhild on Christmas Eve.

But after all this they needed something hot inside them. Simonsen knew of a snug little temperance café; it was Sunday, so the licensed ones were closed. There were no other customers, and the lady behind the counter was not insensible to Simonsen's gallant conversation while he had his coffee and sandwich and Svanhild a cream cake and a sip from Daddy's cup now and again.

"Not a word to Mummy!" Simonsen said with a wink. But Svanhild knew better than to tell Mummy when she and Daddy popped in here and there on their evening walks, and Svanhild had a stick of barley-sugar although Mummy believed it gave little girls worms in their teeth, and Daddy had something to drink which Mummy thought gave him worms in the stomach. But Mummy was always busy and it made her very cross—and Daddy was busy too when he was in the warehouse, and Henry at the office—

[1] Rose-painting: a traditional Norwegian style of decoration.

When people were grown-up they had to work terribly hard. Svanhild knew that.

But after Sunday came Monday and five other gray week-days. Svanhild sat on the floor in the sewing-room and played, for Daddy came back so late in the evenings now that he had no time to take her for a walk. Daddy was cross too, now, she noticed; perhaps because he had so much work to do at the warehouse, or because Mummy had so much work that she hardly had time to get dinner or supper until late. And Henry was cross as well, for ladies had fittings until late at night in the room where he slept, so that he couldn't get to bed. But Svanhild consoled herself with the thought of the wonderful sled she was going to have for Christmas.

On the fifteenth Anton wrote to his son. He was sick of running after jobs in vain. After that he took a calmer view of the future, and had time once more to go out with Svanhild in the evenings and drag her along on her skis in the park; and they talked about the fine sled she was going to have.

But on the morning of the eighteenth, as Simonsen was nailing up a crate of machinery parts, the chief storeman came to tell him that he was wanted on the telephone. It was Sigurd; he was in town. Would his father drop in at the Augustin for coffee—take a couple of hours off that afternoon so that they could have a talk?

"How's Mossa and the children?"

The children were very well. Mossa was in town too; she had a bit of Christmas shopping to do.

"I've just remembered, son—I haven't a chance of getting even an hour off now, with Christmas coming on."

Sigurd said he'd have a word with the manager.

Well, thanks. Love to Mossa.

How like her! Ask him to dinner? Not on your life! Damned if he wouldn't get himself a skinful before he went to that *party*.

"Do you think you must?" Mrs. Carling asked her husband, who was uncorking a bottle of punch.

"Yes, I really think we can stand the old man a glass of punch."

"Well, well, just as you like, dear." Mossa Carling displayed all the double chins at her command. She was not pretty: her eyelids thickened toward the temples, so that her stabbing little gray eyes seemed to creep toward the bridge of her nose; her face was fat and fresh-colored but her mouth small and pinched, with thin lips. Her chest was narrow and cramped, but the lower half of her body was broad and bulky.

She sat in the middle of the plush sofa under the

electric chandelier, whose three lights splendidly illu-
minated the hotel room with its two iron beds, two
mahogany washstands, two bedside tables, the ward-
robe with the mirror, and the two armchairs in front
of the table, on which an ash tray stood on a mat in
the middle of the chenille cloth.

There was a timid knock on the door, and Simonsen stepped warily into the room. He shook hands.

"Well, Sigurd, nice to see you again, my boy. How
are you, Mossa? Glad to see you again too—young and
pretty as ever, I see."

Mossa rang for coffee and poured it out while Sigurd filled the glasses.

While he talked to Sigurd, Simonsen glanced at
his daughter-in-law, who sat mute with a pinched
mouth. Slowly and deviously the conversation turned
toward the purpose of the meeting.

"We may smoke, mayn't we, my dear? Here, Father, have a cigar. Now, about what you said in your
letter. I went up to the office this morning and had a
word with your boss. He agreed with me: you don't
fit in here in town. The work's too hard for a man of
your age. And I can't get you anything else."

Simonsen said nothing. But Mossa took over.

"You must remember that Sigurd's in a subordinate
position himself—in a way, that is. The board of di-
rectors wouldn't like him to keep bothering their
business connections to give you a job. He's done it

three times now, and each time you've lost your position. I must tell you that Sigurd was in quite serious trouble after getting you into this last place, which it seems you've now lost—"

"Yes, I was. No, as I say, you don't fit in here, Father. And you're too old to start anything new. So there's only one way I can help you. I can get you a job at the Mensted works up in Øimark—it's nice easy work. Of course, the wages aren't high: sixty crowns to start with, I believe. But, as I say, I can get you that."

Simonsen was silent.

"Yes, well—that's the only way I can help you," said Sigurd Carling.

"Do you want me to get it for you then, Father?" he asked after a while.

His father cleared his throat once or twice.

"Yes. Well, now. There's one thing, Sigurd—I don't know whether you've heard anything about it, but I'm engaged to be married—to the lady I've been lodging with these last six years. So I shall have to talk this over with Olga first and see what she thinks. Her name's Olga," he explained: "Mrs. Olga Martinsen, a widow."

There was a horribly long pause. Simonsen fidgeted with the tassels on the armchair.

"She's a real, good, respectable, decent person in every way, Olga is. And she's got a big, expanding dressmaking business here in town, so it's quite a question whether she'd care much about moving into the wilds. Her boy's got an office job here, too."

"Is that the lady—" Sigurd spoke very slowly, "—who's said to have a child by you?"

"We've got a little girl, yes; her name's Svanhild— she'll be five in April."

"Oh." This was Mossa. "So you have a daughter by the woman you lodge with—the woman who's such a good, respectable, decent person in every way."

"And so she is—decent and respectable. And hard-working too. And kind."

"Then it's odd, father-in-law—" Mrs. Carling's voice was very sweet and smooth "—that you didn't marry this wonderful Mrs. Martinsen long ago. You had every reason."

"Well, I'll tell you, Mossa my dear." Simonsen perked up as he thought of what to say. "I didn't want to see any wife of mine toiling and slaving so hard, so I waited until I could find something better. But marry her I will. I've promised her that all along, and I'll keep my word as sure as my name's Anton Simonsen."

"Ye—es." Mossa grew sweeter and smoother. "Sixty crowns a month isn't much to marry on, and keep wife and child. And Mrs. Martinsen can hardly hope to build up a very extensive connection in Øimark."

"The worst part of it is this child of yours, Father," said Sigurd. "But no doubt Mrs. Martinsen can be brought to understand the situation, so that we can come to some arrangement."

"You must remember this about that little sister o' yours—about Svanhild. I don't want her to suffer for being illegitimate, and I think you're taking on a big responsibility, Sigurd, if you interfere in this."

Mossa snatched the word from him, and now there was no trace of gentleness in her voice.

"Responsibility! For *your* illegitimate child! That comes well from you, I *must* say! Here's Sigurd offering to get you a position—for the fourth time—in Øimark. To find one here in town is out of the question. If you don't think you can leave town because of your private affairs, you're perfectly free to stay. And if you can find a job and marry on it, we certainly shan't interfere. But naturally Sigurd can't help you in any other way. *His* responsibility, first and foremost, is to his own wife and children."

Mrs. Carling had put on her silk petticoat and draped herself in her new set of furs when on the following morning she climbed the stairs to Mrs. Martinsen's dressmaking establishment in the courtyard off Ruseløk Road. She placed a determined first finger on the bell under Simonsen's dirty visiting card.

The woman who opened the door was small,

plump, and dark. She had pretty blue eyes in a face that was pale and washed-out from sitting indoors.

"Are you Mrs. Martinsen? I'm Mrs. Carling. I wanted to speak to you."

Rather hesitantly Olga opened the door of the nearest room.

"Please come in. I'm sorry there's no fire in here; we work in the other rooms."

Mrs. Carling sailed in and seated herself in the only armchair. The room was furnished as rooms to let usually are. On the chest of drawers, which was covered with a white cloth, the photographs of the late Mrs. Simonsen, of Sigurd, and of herself were conscientiously arrayed—engagement photographs—and two groups of the grandchildren.

"Well now, Mrs. Martinsen—" Olga was now standing over by the chest of drawers, observing the speaker "—there are one or two things I'd very much like to talk to you about. Won't you sit down?"

"Thank you, but I really haven't much time. What was it you wanted, Mrs. Carling?"

"Quite so. I won't keep you. We understand that Mr. Simonsen, my husband's father, has certain obligations toward you. I don't know whether he has made the present situation clear to you?"

"About the new job in Øimark? Oh, yes."

"Oh. Well, as you know, it's quite a modest position, so that for the time being he won't be able to fulfil his obligations to the child—his and yours. My husband and I have therefore decided to offer you—"

"Thank you very much." Olga spoke quickly and curtly. "We don't want to trouble you with our affairs, Mrs. Carling. We've agreed about it, Anton and I. We've agreed to get married now, right away."

"I see. Mrs. Martinsen, I must point out that Mr. Simonsen cannot expect any assistance from my husband—none whatever. He has a large family himself. And for four people to live on sixty crowns a month—I understand you have another child besides Mr. Simonsen's—"

"My boy will stay here. I have a sister in Trondhjem Road he can live with. Our plan was for us to live in Fredrikstad; I could carry on my dressmaking there, and Aton could come down to us on weekends."

"Yes, well, that *sounds* a very sensible idea. But you see, there are more than enough dressmakers in Fredrikstad already, so it's doubtful whether it would pay you to give up your connection here and start all over again there, *Miss* Martinsen!"

Olga jumped.

"*Mrs.* Martinsen, I beg your pardon. That's what you call yourself, of course. Yes, you see my husband and I have been making a few inquiries. You can't be surprised that we should want to know just what sort of person it was he'd taken up with."

Olga gave a puff of scorn.

"And it's the same thing for me, Mrs. Simonsen—I beg your pardon, Mrs. *Carling,* I mean. But it so happens that Anton thinks none the worse of me because my fiancé ran away to America, leaving me to support myself and my boy the best way I could. And he's told me, Anton has, he's said it over and over again: 'I shan't let you down, Olga.' So it don't seem to me it need concern you at all, Mrs. Carling. We shan't trouble you and come running to you—and as your husband hasn't even kept his father's name—"

"My dear Mrs. Martinsen." Mossa waved her hand and displayed all her double chins. "I beg you not to get so excited. I hadn't the least idea of meddling in your affairs. Quite the contrary—I came here with the very best intentions. I simply wanted to make it quite clear to you—in case you imagined that Mr. Simonsen was any sort of catch—that if you do marry him, I believe all you'll gain will be the pleasure of supporting both him and his child. Just think for a moment. My dear father-in-law has never been exactly a model of efficiency, has he? We have no guarantee that he won't be dismissed again as usual. Yes . . . Do you think it will be easy for a man of his age—with a family—to keep on finding new situations? I've come here in a perfectly friendly way to bring you an offer from Mr. Carling. Look, my dear Mrs. Martinsen, up to now you've managed very well without a husband.

Mr. Carling offers you a sum of money—we thought five hundred crowns—to compensate you for losing your lodger so suddenly. Without conditions. You understand that if later my father-in-law is so placed that he can marry we won't stand in the way. As you very rightly say, it doesn't concern us. And as for your little girl, we're prepared to offer her a home with us—"

"Never!" Olga flashed. "Let Svanhild go? That's one thing you can be certain I'll never do."

"Well, well. That's entirely as you wish, of course. You and my father-in-law will naturally please yourselves. If you like to marry on sixty crowns a month—give up your livelihood here and try to start a dressmaking business in Fredrikstad, which I assure you will never succeed . . . What baffles me is why you should want Mr. Simonsen at all. To *marry* him! In your circles people surely aren't so particular as to whether or not you've had some little affair with your lodger. How you could take up with him in the first place . . . You must forgive my saying this, but it's no recommendation in my eyes. Frankly, he's a nasty old man—"

Olga broke in: "Please say no more, Mrs. Carling. But I'll tell you just why I wanted Anton Simonsen. Maybe there *is* one or two things against him. But it didn't take me long to find out that he's a kindhearted man—and there's not too many of that sort about. And as soon as he saw I wanted to make things snug and comfortable for him, he took to me and tidied himself up and behaved himself; and he'd a' done it before, *I* say, if he'd had any kindness or comfort where he come from. Kind and grateful always, Anton's been. And so taken up with Svanhild—almost too much of a good thing, it is—he quite spoils her. I'm fond of Anton, let me tell you, Mrs. Carling."

Mossa stood up and put the tips of her gloved fingers between the lace edges of her muff.

"Ah, well. If you *love* Mr. Simonsen, that's another matter."

Sigurd Carling had a high opinion of his wife's cleverness—he'd heard about it so often that he'd come to believe in it. As Miss Mossa Myhre she had pushed him on and made him the man he was today. Nevertheless, he had his doubts of her being the right person to come to an understanding with Mrs. Martinsen. She had very strict views, and this Olga creature had had two children in a rather irregular manner. And Mossa could make herself most unpleasant. So afterward he regretted having let her go: it had been a stupid thing to do. For an arrangement of some sort there must be. If his father were to move to Fredrikstad with a wife and child whom he couldn't support, it was as clear as daylight what would happen: Sigurd and his wife would never be safe from appeals for help, along with all the other kinds of bother his father always caused. And endless trouble with Mossa.

The matter had to be settled, and at once, before the old man had time to play them any tricks. Sigurd went to the Hercules works and ordered two new turbines, and in passing said a word or two about his father. It was arranged that Simonsen should leave for good on Christmas Eve, so that he might go home with them for the holiday.

Afterward, he too went to see Mrs. Martinsen.

Olga was tear-stained when Simonsen came home at dinnertime. Carling had been there. He'd been quite nice; he had asked to see Svanhild and taken her on his lap, and told her she should have something special for Christmas. Afterward he had talked to Olga. It was about her debts: she owed rent, as well as sums here and there among the tradespeople. And she had accepted his money. Besides that, he had promised her fifteen crowns a month for Svanhild; that meant something steady coming in, and she had Henry too, who wouldn't be able to support himself for a while —fifteen crowns a month, he'd said, for the time being: "until my father has become self-supporting and can marry you." Olga sat on Simonsen's knee and cried; he was in the armchair in that cold room, in front of the chest of drawers with its family photographs. She cried, and he patted her.

"Oh, Anton, I don't know! What else could I a' done? If he won't help you there's nothing else for it. And I could see he wouldn't—not in any other way. If they set themselves against us, we should never make a go of it in Fredrikstad, you see—"

She blew her nose and wiped her eyes. And had another fit of crying.

"We got to accept it—you got to accept a lot of things when you're poor."

But to go home with Sigurd and Mossa for Christmas was one thing Simonsen would not do. They tempted him with a Christmas tree and grandchildren and goose and beer and spirits and pickled brawn, but the old man stood firm: he wanted to spend Christmas with Olga and the children. The most they managed to get from Simonsen was his promise to go down the day after Christmas Day. Sigurd had given him twenty-five crowns, so it was as well to get him out of town rather than let him loaf about there with money in his pocket until the New Year. Far better for the old boy to have his Christmas drinks with them, under supervision.

When Simonsen came home the evening before Christmas Eve, he had the new sled under his arm. Humming away in a deep bass voice he lit the lamp in his own room and unpacked his parcels.

There were drinks—aqua vitae and punch and

brandy, and sweet port for Olga; so with a drop of beer they'd do all right. A pipe for Henry—it hadn't cost much; it was really just to show the boy he hadn't forgotten him, and it was a manly sort of thing to have. All the same he was pretty well broke now; the blouse material for Olga cost only 1 crown 45 øre, but then he'd bought her a brooch too, for 3.75, which looked more like ten crowns' worth. Simonsen took it out of its little box; he was sure she'd like it. He wanted to buy some little trifle for Miss Abrahamsen too—just a souvenir. Something quite small—he could afford that.

And then the sled, of course. Simonsen took the cloth off the table, unpacked the sled, and put it on display.

"Come and have a look, Olga love," he called into the sewing-room.

"What is it? I'm busy."

Simonsen moved the lamp over to the table.

"What do you think Svanhild will say to this, eh, Olga?"

"Mind the veneer, Anton!" and she spread newspaper under the sled and the lamp. "Yes, that's lovely—that's a beautiful sled."

"And look!" Simonsen unbuckled the cushion so that Olga could see all the rose-painting. "The cushion was extra."

"H'm. Must have been dear."

"Five crowns and twenty-five øre with the cushion," Simonsen answered briskly.

"Yes, well, that's a lot of money to spend on a thing like that, Anton. For such a little girl—she'd have been just as happy with a plainer one." Olga sighed.

"Oh, but now we got a little ready money handy, it's fun to give nice things. You've settled your debts and that. I bought something for my sweetheart too—" and he nudged her. "Run and fetch a couple of glasses, Olga—I've got some port. You must taste it and see how you like it—I bought it on your account mostly."

Olga glanced at the many bottles on the chest of drawers and sighed a little. Then she fetched the glasses.

It was late on Christmas Eve when work finished at Mrs. Martinsen's. But at last all was done. Henry had gone off to deliver the last of the completed sewing, and Olga and Miss Abrahamsen had cleared away everything else, heaping it on the chairs and table in the sewing-room. Before she left, Miss Abrahamsen was given coffee and pastries and from Simonsen a bottle of eau-de-Cologne.

Then Olga went into the sitting-room. She cleared the magazines off the table, and materials and half-made garments off the chairs, and picked up pins and buttons to drop them into the glass bowls on the console table. And she lit the candles on the Christmas tree, which she had decorated the night before.

Svanhild and Henry and Simonsen came in; the grown-ups sat down on the plush chairs, but Svanhild skipped and danced and rejoiced; she caught sight of the sled and shrieked with delight, then ran back to the tree again, not knowing what to do with herself for joy. Simonsen beamed and Olga smiled, though her eyes were sadly red; Simonsen had glanced at them several times during the afternoon. It would be the limit if she started to cry on this of all evenings, when they were going to have such a nice time.

He fetched his presents, smiling mischievously: she wouldn't think the blouse material was much of a gift. Then he brought out the eau-de-Cologne; for he had yielded to the temptation of doing things in style when he went into the fifty-øre bazaar after something for Miss Abrahamsen. There was also a cup to hold Olga's ball of wool when she knitted, and a little matchbox that looked like silver for Henry. The boy shook hands and laid pipe and box down by the window, where he had been lounging in a chair. But then came the brooch.

"All those was sort of practical things, Olga; you must have a little trifle just for pleasure, too."

Olga picked up the brooch and her eyes filled with tears.

"Such a lot of things, Anton!"

Simonsen threw out his hand in a magnificent gesture.

"You must think of me when you wear it, Olga love."

"Oh, I will, Anton."

"And what about that box that came for Svanhild?"

Olga fetched it. On it was written: "To little Miss Svanhold, % Mrs. Martinsen's dressmaking establishment." Olga opened it. The card inside bore the inscription: "Merry Christmas!" It was Sigurd Carling's card. With it was a doll—but what a doll!

It had curly yellow hair and eyes that opened and shut. It was dressed in a white coat and white fur cap, and carried a little pair of skates over its arm—that was the most marvelous thing of all. Svanhild was speechless, but Simonsen talked and talked; he and the child were equally enraptured with the doll.

"Mummy must keep it for you—you'd better only play with it on Sundays."

"He's a good fellow, you know, Sigurd is," he said to Olga, who was bringing in the glasses and the jug of hot water. "It's what I always say: Sigurd's all right at heart—it's that damned hag of his who puts him up to things, for he's a good chap."

Simonsen mixed a toddy and Olga had port. Svanhild too was given a little drop of the sweet wine in her own glass as she sat on Daddy's lap.

"Come along, Henry, and mix yourself a toddy. You're a man now, you know."

Henry rose rather reluctantly, not looking at Simonsen. He had hard, pale eyes in a white, freckled face, and he looked thin and slight in his grown-up clothes.

"Well, *skål*, everybody! Isn't this jolly! Eh, Olga love?"

"Yes," she said, and bit her lip. Tears came into her eyes. "If only we knew what next Christmas was going to be like."

Simonsen lit his cigar. He looked troubled.

"Aren't you going to try your pipe, Henry, my boy? You'll find some tobacco on my chest of drawers if you haven't any yourself."

"No, thanks," said Henry.

"Yes, next Christmas," said Olga, fighting with her tears.

"Hard to say when you don't know," Simonsen said. He leaned back in his chair. "Good cigar, this. Drink up, Olga. Yes, well, perhaps we'll all be celebrating Christmas together among the country bumpkins. I hear they have great goings-on at Christmas up in Øimark. I think you'd like the country, Olga. When you want a Christmas tree, all you got to do is walk out of the door and cut one. Not bad! How'd you like that, Svanhild—going out into the woods with your daddy to cut down a Christmas tree—and then drag it home on your sled, eh?"

Svanhild nodded, radiant.

"And Henry would get time off from the office and spend Christmas with us."

Henry smiled slightly—scornfully.

"Wouldn't that be fun, Svanhild—going to the station to meet Henry? Would you like it if you and Daddy and Mummy lived on a big farm with cows and horses and pigs and roosters and hens and all? And then kind Sigurd, who gave you your doll—he's got a little girl about your age, and a boy just a bit bigger, and a tiny, tiny baby; you could go into town and play with them."

"While I have tea with that stuck-up daughter-in-law of yours, I s'pose! That's the idea, eh, Anton?"

"Oh, well—I don't think that would be necessary—"

"How can you go on talking such nonsense!" Olga laughed—and then burst out crying.

"Oh, now Olga, what are you crying for, love? Why do you take it like that?"

"How do you expect me to take it? Am I supposed to be pleased when that woman throws it in my face that Henry's father made a fool of me, and that now you're leaving me too? And me and my children—my by-blows—we're left with the disgrace. Perhaps you think like they do—you think it serves me right to sit here and make clothes for all the girls you have fun and games with. Just as if it was all right for people to treat me as they choose. Yes, yes—good enough for me. I ought to a' known what you was all like; soon's you get your own way with a poor woman it's love you and leave you—thanks and good-by!"

"But Olga, my dear!"

"Ah, it's nothing to you. No, you can move out into the country, you can, and start all over again with your sozzling and your girls—like you was doing when I found you. And my God, a nice fool I was to give in to you."

"Olga, Olga—remember the children!"

"Ho, they hear enough about it, you may be sure, in the yard and on the stairs. So they might just as well hear it from me too."

"It's Christmas Eve, Olga. Remember that, please," Simonsen said solemnly.

Olga wept quietly with her head on the table. Simonsen laid his hand on her shoulder.

"Now Olga, you know very well—you know very well how fond I am of you. And there's Svanhild—d'you really think I'd forget my own, innocent little girl? Trust me, Olga; I won't let you down or deceive you—I'll keep my promise to you."

"Why, you poor man—" Olga sat up and blew her nose. "That's not for you to decide."

"But you must remember one thing, Olga—" Si-

monsen laid one arm round her neck and held Svanhild with the other, straightened himself, and stuck
out his stomach. "There's One Above—one greater
than either Sigurd or Mossa—who *does* decide—for
us all."

"Now I think we ought to sing a carol," he said a
little later. He took a gulp of toddy and cleared his
throat. 'The Joy of Christmas'—let's have that; Svanhild knows it, I know. Sing out, now, Svanhild love."

Svanhild sang joyfully, and Simonsen growled too,
leaving off when the notes went too high, but beginning again with every verse. Presently Olga joined in
with a voice hoarse from weeping. Henry alone did
not sing.

Then came the last morning. In Olga's room the
alarm clock rang, but Simonsen lay dozing on in the
darkness—it was so cold getting up. And everything
was dreary and comfortless. That he should have to
get up in the cold and go away—away from everything.

Never, in any place where he had lived, had he had
so comfortable a bed as this, with eiderdown both under and over him.

Olga opened the door, and by the light shining
through from her room she set down the tray she was
carrying, lit the lamp, and took the tray over to the
bed; on it were coffee and rolls.

"You'll have to get moving now, Anton."

"Yes, yes—I s'pose so."

Simonsen sighed. He drew her down on to the edge of the bed and stroked her—stroked her cheek and arm and breast and hips, as he drank the coffee and dunked the rolls in it.

"This is splendid coffee, my love. Won't you have a drop too?"

"No, I'd better go and get a bit of breakfast ready for you."

Simonsen crawled out of bed, dressed, and packed the last of his belongings. Then he locked both his boxes and went into Olga's room.

He stood by the bed where Svanhild lay asleep, looking down at her with his hands in his pockets. "My Svanhild . . ."

He peeped into the sitting-room too; it was pitch-dark and icy cold. Henry had gone off to Nordmarka with some friends on Christmas morning. Simonsen pottered about in there for a while, and in the darkness knocked against Svanhild's Christmas tree, so that the little tinsel balls tinkled together. Who knew —who knew whether he would ever come back here again?

He returned to Olga's room; it was nice and warm in there. Places were laid at the lower end of the long table where Olga and Miss Abrahamsen worked during the day. On the white cloth were brawn and beer and spirits and all the rest, and over it the lamp shone peacefully, humming softly as it burned. A light fell on Svanhild, asleep in her little bed, with her pretty hair spread over the pillow. His little, little girl . . .

There was a sweet, cosy warmth from Olga's bed, which was unmade, the covers thrown back from the hollow where she had lain. How good his life had been here with Olga and Svanhild! His eyes filled with tears; he let them run without drying them, so that Olga should see them. His pouchy, bluish-red cheeks were quite wet when Olga came in with the coffee.

"We'd better have breakfast," she said.

"Yes, we'd better. What about Svanhild? D'you think she'd like to come to the station, just for the sleigh ride?"

"I thought of that, Anton, but it's so dark and cold outside. But I might wake her now, so she can have a cup of coffee with us."

She went over to the bed and gently shook the child.

"Svanhild, would you like to get up now and have coffee with Mummy and Daddy?"

Svanhild blinked, sitting in her nightgown on Simonsen's lap. The coffee had roused her a little, but she was still quiet and subdued because the grownups were.

"Where are you going, Daddy?"

"Why, to Fredrikstad, don't you remember?"

"When are you coming back?"

"Oh, well—I expect you'll be down to see me first."

"In the country, like you talked about?"

"That's it."

"You'll be able to toboggan with me again there, won't you, Daddy?"

"Yes, that's right—I'll be able to toboggan with you again there."

The doorbell rang. Olga looked out: the sleigh had come. The carter's boy took Simonsen's boxes and went.

Simonsen kissed Svanhild, and having got up, he stood for a little with her on his arm.

"Now you must be a good girl, mind, and do as you're told while Daddy's away!"

"Yes, I will," said Svanhild.

Olga went into the kitchen to turn off the stove, as Svanhild was to be alone at home; then came in again and stood with her hand on the lamp screw.

"Well, Anton—"

He gave Svanhild a smacking kiss, laid her down in her bed, and covered her up.

"Bye-bye then, Svanhild love."

Olga put out the lamp, and they left the room. In the hall he put his arms round her and pressed her to him. They kissed.

In the sleigh they sat in silence as they jolted down through the darkness of early morning. And they still had nothing to say to each other as they wandered together round the cold, bleak station hall. But she followed at his heels when he bought his ticket and despatched his trunk; she stood behind him, a small figure in black, square in her thick outer clothes.

Then they wandered into the waiting-room and sat looking up at the clock.

"We started in good time, didn't we?" said Olga.

"Yes, we did. Best thing when you're going on a journey. Shame you had to get up so early, though, when it's a holiday."

"Oh, well," said Olga. "Perhaps we'd better go along and take a seat for you on the train."

Simonsen put his things into a smoking-compartment. He stood at the window while she remained down on the platform.

"Mind you, write often, Olga, and tell me how you're getting on."

"Yes—and you too, Anton."

Porters began slamming the carriage doors along the train. Olga got up on the step, and they kissed again.

"Thanks for everything, Olga love."

"And thanks to you, Anton. Good journey!"

The engine whistled—a jerk ran through the train, and it began to move. Olga and Simonsen pulled out their handkerchiefs and waved to each other for as long as the handkerchiefs could be seen.

The train swished away in the first pale light of dawn—past the Bekkelag villas, past Nordstrand and Ljan. There were lights in the windows here and there. Below the railway line the fjord could be glimpsed, ice-gray, with black islands on it.

Oh, it was dreary . . . Simonsen was alone in the compartment, smoking his cigar and looking out of the window. Farms and woods came up and swam past —gray-brown fields with strips of snow along their edges—black woods.

By now Olga would be at home again. What would she be doing? Dressing Svanhild, probably. Olga had to work today, so she'd said. Svanhild would sit on the floor by the window, playing with the waste scraps. Now she had no Daddy to go tobogganing with in the Palace Park.

The snug room with its two warm, white beds. And the lamp, and the sewing everywhere, and the scraps on the floor which one waded through. Svanhild over by the window—his own, precious child. He could see her sitting there so quietly with her little affairs. Now and then a Miss Hellum or someone came in and gave her sweets. She'd miss her Daddy, Svanhild would.

It was wrong. It was all wrong.

For a moment the wrongness of it struck a spark inside him and smarted and burned through all that life had left of Anton Simonsen's heart.

"Svanhild love, my own little Svanhild . . ." he whimpered.

But he thrust the thought away.

That innocent little girl, who was so good—so very good. Surely life would turn out well for her?

He wiped his eyes. There must be One Above who decided these things. That must be his consolation: that there was One who decided . . .

A NOTE ON THE AUTHOR

SIGRID UNDSET was born at Kalundborg, Denmark, on May 20, 1882. From 1899 to 1909, she was a clerk in an office in Christiania. She began publishing stories in 1907, and won resounding success with the novel *Jenny* in 1912, the year of her marriage to Anders C. Svarstad (annulled in 1925). Having undergone a religious crisis, she joined the Roman Catholic Church in 1925. Between 1920 and 1922, Mme Undset had published the three volumes (*The Bridal Wreath, The Mistress of Husaby,* and *The Cross*) of her great fourteenth-century historical novel *Kristin Lavransdatter,* which soon made her world-famous. This major work was followed (1925–7) by the four sections (*The Axe, The Snake Pit, In the Wilderness,* and *The Son Avenger*) of her other magnificent historical panorama, *The Master of Hestviken,* and she was awarded the Nobel Prize for Literature in 1928. She wrote many other novels, as well as short stories, essays, and poems, and translated Icelandic sagas. Having lived in the United States for some time in the 1940's, she returned to Norway after the end of the Second World War and died at Lillehammer, Norway, on June 10, 1949.

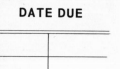

DATE DUE